SO MANY WITNESSES

SO MANY WITNESSES

*The Story of the
Churches' Fellowship for Psychical and Spiritual Studies
1953 – 1993*

by

BARBARA BUNCE

CFPSS

First Impression – 1993

ISBN 0 902666 37 1

Copyright © Barbara Bunce 1993

Published by
The Churches' Fellowship for Psychical and Spiritual Studies
The Rural Workshop, South Road, North Somercotes,
Nr Louth, Lincolnshire.

Printed in Wales by
John Penry Press, Swansea

DEDICATION

*To all those who have gone before us
and whose devotion and example have
helped us on the Way –*

*"With so many witnesses in a great cloud
on every side of us..."
Heb. 12:1 (Jer. Bible)*

"In my opinion it is important that Christian thought should take account of the results of psychical research and of super-normal phenomena, as it seems probable that new light on human personality may come from this source" –
December 1954 – W.R. Matthews, Dean of St. Paul's

"Add to your faith virtue; and to virtue knowledge"
2 Peter 1:5 (KJV)

CFPSS *Motto:*
"TO FAITH ADD KNOWLEDGE"

Acknowledgements

I have to thank so many people who have contributed in some way to the writing of this history; in talking to me, writing to me, passing on manuscripts or printed material, sharing ideas, thoughts or memories, not to mention the countless contributors to the Fellowship journals and records. I would especially like to thank Julian Drewett for his support, assistance and encouragement throughout; and Martin Israel, Michael Perry and Maurice Frost for reading the manuscript and making valuable comments. There have, of course, been many others; not being very sensitive I have only occasionally been aware of their benign presence, but I thank them too.

Contents

Introduction	i
1. York 1989	1
2. Foundations and the First Ten Years	9
3. The CFPSS and the Hereafter	21
4. The CFPSS and the Ministry of Healing	28
5. The CFPSS and Psychical Research	34
6. The CFPSS and Prayer and Mysticism	41
7. The CFPSS and the Churches	48
8. The CFPSS and Christian Parapsychology	55
9. Fellow Members and Pilgrims	62
10. An Ongoing Fellowship	72
Appendix A	84
Appendix B	86
Chapter Notes	88
Index	92

Introduction

In the production of this book I have felt so strongly that I was writing on behalf of many other people that, had I allowed myself to be too influenced by this, the task might have become impossible, for it is a generally accepted fact that a committee cannot produce a book. I have to state at the outset, therefore, that this is only one picture of the Churches' Fellowship for Psychical and Spiritual Studies; another writer might have represented it quite differently. In my awareness of this I have tried to be as factual as possible about the inauguration and development of the CFPSS, using as my sources minutes of meetings, reports of conferences, records and accounts in the "Quarterly Review", the "Christian Parapsychologist" and regional newsletters, rather than relying upon memories, either my own or those of other members, except where a touch of colour seemed justifiable.

There are two main areas in which I feel that others might have written this history differently. First there will be for many a feeling of disappointment that certain notable characters and personalities are not included by name, or, if included, are not given more space. I am only too well aware of several such, and there will be many more who will be thought of as serious omissions, either because they are remembered for a great contribution, or even perhaps as protagonists in controversy. However, before I started there was an agreed length; then, in dealing with the great mass of material available, it seemed best to divide it up in the way that the chapter headings indicate. Working within the limits prescribed and the divisions chosen, some foreshortenings and omissions were inevitable.

The second area in which there may be disappointment felt by some lies in the emphasis, or lack of it, given to different aspects of our studies. The CFPSS, not unlike the Church, has groups of members who see quite differently from the other groupings as to the raison d'être and function of the parent

i

body to which they belong. Nowhere is this difference felt more strongly than in connection with the question of communication from or with the departed. For many this has been the issue over which they have felt most in need of the understanding and support of a body such as the CFPSS. That is, a body which recognises the inherent possibility of such a phenomenon, its reality, and great value in certain circumstances, while accepting the need to analyse, evaluate the genuine, and identify deception and wrongness when that is appropriate; all this needing to be held within a Christian commitment and discipline. Perhaps the CFPSS approach is best exemplified in a recent book by Beryl Statham, one of its most dedicated members, in which she weaves together her own and others' experiences on a Christian journey of discovery and growth in this most difficult field.[1] Certainly this was the path by which the early members and founders came to recognise the need for a society such as the CFPSS.

At the same time, a large proportion of CFPSS members believe that other spiritual concerns need equal if not more attention; and indeed many members prefer to leave the question of the departed on one side, or to let it be wrapped comprehensively in the concept of the Holy Spirit having the care of all souls, departed or here on earth, omitting all idea of individuality until the time comes to understand more than is possible in a mortal state. For those of this way of thinking, their major preoccupations in the Fellowship have been with healing, prayer, meditation and a deepening life in Christ.

This division in approach to the subject, within one organisation, has been compared to trying to drive two horses, each pulling in a different direction. Yet it seems that neither CFPSS horse has really wanted to leave the other, nor, most importantly, to pull away from the shared driver. This, I believe, is the element which has continued to ensure cohesion between those of differing opinions. All turn to one overall source of inspiration and direction, Jesus Christ, and his Holy Spirit, and in that belief all differences are kept in proportion, to be dealt with, clarified, healed, in God's good time.

Perhaps the differences met in this way keep us a living organism. Certainly because of our varied understandings we are able to meet a wider spectrum of enquiries than if we all held to one uniform interpretation of our experiences. From the beginning our founders saw bridge-building, with fellow Christians, or with those who have lost their faith, or with doctors, scientists and theologians, as a vital part of CFPSS work. This theme of bridge-building, as will be seen, is frequently stressed as representing a great need in our present age. Now as I write, just before our annual conference in Plymouth, which has "Bridges" as its theme, it seems suitable to express the hope that this history will itself act as a bridge, between those of differing understanding, and between past, present and future, so that the CFPSS can go forward confidently to make the best contribution possible in the testing times to come.

Barbara Bunce
EXETER. August, 1992.

CHAPTER 1
York – 1989

In the ancient city of York, near the magnificent Minster, and Roman, Viking, mediaeval and other historical sites, lies the York campus of the College of Ripon and York, St. John. Here, on Friday, 1st September, 1989, 150 members of the Churches' Fellowship for Psychical and Spiritual Studies, with 20 visitors, came together for the Annual Conference and General Meeting. The conference was to last for the weekend.

Until 1981, Annual Conferences had, by tradition, been held in London. It had then become apparent that London was no longer the accessible and desirable destination that it had once been; and Digby Stuart College, Roehampton, where, over the latter years, the Annual Conferences had been held, was becoming increasingly difficult for members to reach from the main London stations.

The Fellowship had therefore begun to seek other conference venues which would make the Annual General Meeting available to as many members as possible. Love for the history of the Christian church from which it had sprung, and to which it belonged, directed the choice of location towards Cathedral cities. Eventually it had become the custom that the Annual Conference would alternate between London and other suitable cities around the country. Canterbury, Chichester, Lincoln and Worcester had been visited in 1981, 1983, 1985 and 1987, respectively; and now, in 1989, the Fellowship was meeting in York.

So members gathered, with a sense of anticipation, for a weekend in an important and lovely city, embedded in Christian history, and with a programme of speakers including the Archbishop of York himself, the Most Rev. John Habgood. Added to which there would be the opportunity to meet old friends, renew acquaintances from previous conferences, and to meet and make new friends, all with the common interest which had brought them to the College.

A society such as the CFPSS needs occasionally to look back, always to consider the present, and frequently to look to the future. The publication of this history is planned for 1993, the fortieth year since the Fellowship's foundation, a milestone which is to be celebrated in the city and cathedral of Durham. This anniversary seems to be the natural occasion to establish a sense of what the Fellowship has so far become, to trace its origins and early days, and finally look ahead to see what it has still to do. It seems suitable to take the conference in York as a marker for the current position for, while all were agreed that there was something special about the occasion, it was still typical of a CFPSS gathering at any regional day or half-day conference, or branch meeting, with the added intensity of the size of the York gathering and its splendid setting. Thus was the essential character of the CFPSS blended with a sense of place and occasion.

The task of assessing that essential character, for one who has been a member for a great many years, necessitates taking a step aside to observe and listen to the newer members, the enquirers, those seeking answers to questions, or strength and comfort in loss and pain.

A common thread runs through such reactions, a sense of coming home, of finding a safe haven, and yet at the same time a feeling of adventure and excitement at new horizons opening. Part of that common basis, too, must be the recognition of that something within the human personality which is deeper than the prevailing materialistic concepts of science and medicine; and added to this would be loyalty to the Christian faith, seeking permission to be aware of these non-material factors and to study them within the meaning of the psychical and the spiritual, and yet never to deny or decry our Christian origins.

Within this framework of Christian commitment and exploration, the majority of those attending the York conference could celebrate their membership and the occasion, while listening and ministering to those who had come with deeper needs, many perhaps on their first voyage of discovery.

One such had first come to the Fellowship earlier in the year.

For four years she had lived in sadness after a family tragedy and was, as she said herself, at a low ebb. Membership of the Fellowship had brought new meaning into her life, security and peace, and a revived faith. At York she felt this new contentment was capped and sealed as she heard brilliant and spiritually gifted speakers, on matters of life and death, and met ordinary members, all with experiences and gifts to share.

Another new member, struggling to recover from years of shattering losses, had this to say afterwards. "I want to thank all the members of the team who made the annual conference at York possible, and the wonderful experience that, without doubt, it was. The help I had from certain individuals, and particularly the spiritual fellowship I found within the group of people to which I was drawn, was beyond anything I had imagined. Coming to York was a great privilege. My faith and love have been strengthened, restored and renewed, and for this I thank all who made such a great effort to help us all at York."

Such seekers and others could be observed, talking quietly in a small group or to an individual as, away from the public platform and talks, the work of ministry through listening, sensitivity, insight and intuition was unobtrusively carried out. An early founding member who always summarised the work of the CFPSS, as she saw it, as "to comfort the sorrowing and to heal the sick" would have been deeply touched, and indeed must praise God from her place in the Communion of Saints.

Joy and lively conversation also feature very greatly in such gatherings, so much so that in York several people attending a teachers' conference being held at the same time, meeting members at meals or in the social rooms, became very interested in the society, wishing they could transfer to the CFPSS conference, and taking away some of our literature. A good witness it seemed.

However, to follow the conference in sequence, first came the settling in and greetings over tea, before gathering for the first talk. At the back of the conference room would be the keen readers clustered around the long book stall where the General Secretary and helpers presided over a wide selection of books relevant to CFPSS studies. Most of these would be acceptable to most Christians, especially those dealing with Christian spirituality in all its forms; some might prove more controversial, since not all Christians agree on everything; none would be on aspects of the more questionable or darker side of the psychical field, except for Christian-inspired books on the ministry of deliverance, and these would come under the label of Christian healing, of which there would be many examples.

As members settled for the first talk, quiet descended with a sense of focussed attention. The Chairman of the Fellowship, the Ven. Michael Perry, Archdeacon of Durham, inaugurated the conference with prayer, and then introduced the first speaker, the President, the Rev. Dr Martin Israel. The theme of the conference was "Religious Experience"; and who better than such a brilliant mystic, combining such disparate disciplines as pathology and theology, counselling and spiritual direction, to lead us into the subject of his first talk, "The Knowledge of God". Quoting St. Augustine: "Our hearts are restless until they find their rest in thee", he spoke of our need to know God in the inner quietness, where the Spirit may reveal truth and take us to the Father. God is the creative part of each individual, and to be truly alive we have to know him. All that he makes is good, and he has given us free will.

After dinner, despite the sense of occasion which was inseparable from listening to the next speaker, the Archbishop of York, speaking to us on his own ground as it were, the Most Rev. John Habgood paved the way for his own great scholarship with a disarming recognition of his lack of expertise in our subject and of the importance of the work of the Fellowship, particularly in a world more often interested in psychic phenomena than in orthodox theology. He recognised, too, the frustration felt by many when orthodox religion seemed to turn a deaf ear to what is being said out of some very special experiences; and he welcomed the opportunity to reflect with us.

Then, speaking to his title, "Experience and Belief", he led us through an exposition of some theological resources to use as a framework for our studies, these drawn from the work of an American theologian, George Lindbeck, in his book "The Nature of Doctrine". The aim of such a framework would be to enable the building of bridges between different cultural frameworks, the most difficult being that between science and theology, at which he, Dr Habgood, had worked for 40 years. Yet he acknowledged that bridge-building with psychic experiences might be even more difficult because it belongs, on the whole, to a tradition which has been rejected by mainstream intellectual scholarship.

It seems relevant at this point, in assessing the history of the CFPSS, to quote in full Dr Habgood's closing remarks, pointing as they do to a possible path for our future work.

"Where and how to build the bridges, I would have thought, ought to be a main concern of this Fellowship. We all know the attempts that there have been at bridge-building through emphasis on controlled scientific experiments in psychic matters, but again one has to recognise that the results of this do not, at the moment, seem to have been sufficiently convincing to cause real changes in attitudes.

"The thought I want to leave with you is that perhaps orthodox Christian theology might be a better bridge. It can serve as a bridge, however, only if it pays proper attention to the unknown depths in its own tradition. One of the problems is that orthodox Christian theology can appear sometimes in a very superficially, rigidly defined guise. If, as I have suggested, we see it much more in this "community" context, as a community of people endeavouring to make sense of their experience at all levels in the light of a tradition which has a solidity and validity which has proved itself over many centuries, then I believe, in the long run, some viable bridges can be built. It seems to me that a particular rôle for your Fellowship lies in opening up some of these depths, while remaining part of that tradition of rational religious thought which links us with the best minds both in the past and in the present."

So, as the Ven. Michael Perry said, in thanking the Archbishop, we had been stimulated intellectually but also confronted by a challenge, which we needed to take on board as a Fellowship, a challenge for the years ahead.

Part of the response to that challenge undoubtedly lies in new work and perhaps new methods of work to be developed in the years to come; but in the context of the history now being considered it seems that a wealth of work already accomplished needs to be studied anew and brought into whatever totality of effort lies before us. Perhaps as that earlier work is studied in succeeding chapters it may become apparent how much there is to be drawn upon for future students and bridge-builders. In the words of Michael Perry, in a book which is in itself a wise and comprehensive guide to the subject: "In religion and spirituality, in every human science, and in psychical research, we stand on the shoulders of others in order to try to see further than they have been able to."[1]

The next day, Saturday, began with the pre-breakfast meditation. The first speaker after breakfast exemplified the value of more recent developments in the field of psychical and spiritual studies. Mr David Lorimer,[2] Chairman of the United Kingdom branch of the International Association for Near-Death Studies, gave a fascinating and erudite talk on "Near-Death Experiences", skilfully linking his subject with the two previous speakers. He quoted Dr Raymond Moody, the pioneer in the field,[3] who told of a patient emerging from a near-death experience and saying: "God wanted to know what was in my heart, not my head"; and he pointed out that NDEs do give some degree of scientific proof, and that they are bridges involving both psychic and spiritual dimensions.

In his second talk to the conference, the Rev. Dr Martin Israel, under the title "The Purpose of Religion", emphasised that we are the instruments of God's love, which was far more important than being, in the currently fashionable term, channels. Religion plays its part in providing a Way to follow that directive, which must involve helping non-Christians as much as fellow Christians. Thus, in the discipline God has given us, we become the priesthood of humanity. So another inspiring challenge was given to us, reinforcing our understanding that, rewarding as membership of the Fellowship may be, it is no easy option.

After lunch, in such a place as York, there was no difficulty in finding historical and religious interest and inspiration during the free time available. Then came the Annual General Meeting with its business and reports of the work of the preceding year.

Finally after dinner came a splendid and most appropriate talk from Mr John Mitchell, a local member, historian and retired schoolmaster, on "Ghosts of an Ancient City". This was informative as well as humorous, and left questions to be pondered on.

On the last morning, Sunday, an "Any Questions" session was held, when members could bring up points on which they felt they needed further help or elucidation. Some of the questions came from the depths of sorrow, and dealt with such areas of pain as are involved when there has been an unexpected or premature death, and a way forward is seen to be needed for those who have died as well as those left behind.[4] This weaving of pastoral care with the intellectual considerations of theology and philosophy, or the blending of the rational and the experiential, of logic and intuition, is typical of much of the work of the CFPSS.

The last occasion of the conference, as of all annual conferences, was the Eucharist. This was held in the College Chapel. Canon John Smith, a long-term and faithful officer of the Fellowship, especially involved in the ministry of healing and in leading pilgrimages, presided, assisted by the Ven. Michael Perry. It was a memorable and uplifting service. However, perhaps it needs to be said that the Fellowship is not exclusively Anglican in its leadership or membership. It is true that the Anglican branch of Christianity seems most able to accept and hold this sort of liberal, questioning approach, and the majority of members are from the Anglican church. The society is, however inter-denominational, and Methodists, Church of Scotland, Roman Catholic and representatives of many other churches enrich its membership.

So came the final exchanges over lunch, and then the departure to destinations near and far. Those who wanted to be able to hear the talks again were able to take taped copies away with them or resolve to hire them later via the Head Office. New friends and sources of help would have exchanged names and addresses. There would be an account of the conference to look forward to in the next edition of the "Quarterly Review", together with a full Report of the Annual General Meeting.[5] That Report fulfils the obligation of the Fellowship as a registered charity with a formal constitution and clearly defined aims and objects. In this way members who are not able to be present may keep abreast of what is being done on their behalf, and object if they so wish, certainly to express their opinions, via the two journals, "The Quarterly

Review" and "The Christian Parapsychologist", or directly to any officer or council member. The society is a democratic one.

Perhaps the words of the Ven. Michael Perry, closing his Chairman's report, provide a suitable conclusion to this introduction to the Fellowship, as it was in 1989. "So there is plenty going on and planned. The Fellowship is in good heart; I believe it is also in good hands. It is certainly in *God's* hands, which is all that really matters. We are a Christian body committed to serving God with all our faculties – including the psychic faculty. We believe that God made us with these talents, abilities and faculties, and that if we can use them and develop them to His glory, we shall be doing His will and pleasing Him. May that long continue to be the case, and may God bless us in the doing of it!"

So the CFPSS continues, a society of committed Christians, aware of what they gain from their membership but striving always to make that membership fruitful, in service and contribution to contemporary thinking and religion.

When and how did it all begin?

CHAPTER 2

Foundations and the First Ten Years

The first official meeting of the CFPSS was held on 10th November, 1953, with the tentative title of the Churches' Fellowship for Psychic Investigation. Obviously such a meeting was the outcome of many previous contacts and much thought and consultation, reflecting the years of research and conviction on the part of the six people present. There had in fact been ample opportunity for well over a hundred years for the sort of study or research involved. Reputable organisations, with memberships drawn from academic, scientific, and theological circles of the highest standing had been in existence since Victorian times. Of these the Society for Psychical Research, and the London Spiritualist Alliance (later to become the College for Psychic Studies) were typical.

The fact that organised spiritualism was so much a part of the process of psychical research had to be accepted. A large proportion of gifted sensitives, and those with a gift of healing, had had nowhere else to go for explanation, acceptance and use of their gifts. Not all wanted this process to become part of a new religio/philosophic system, and some remained quite independent. However, for the majority a place for such gifts could only be found under the label of spiritualism (which, like "the Church", included a wide range of beliefs, some mainly secular). As time went on, so widespread had become the interest in the spiritual implications of this type of phenomenon, among clergy as well as lay people (reasons for which will be considered in Chapter 3), that it could be said:

"The 1920 Lambeth Conference, for example, studied the relationship of the Christian faith to Spiritualism and related subjects, such as Christian Science and Theosophy. Although the Conference recognised some shortcomings and apparent weaknesses associated with Spiritualism, its popularity did not wane within Anglican circles. Eventually, in 1935 the Dean of Rochester, Francis Underhill, moved the following resolution at the Church Assembly:

'That in view of the growth of Spiritualism among the clergy and communicant laity of the Church, the Assembly respectfully requests their Graces the Archbishops to appoint a commission to investigate the matter and to report to the Assembly.' (Resolution 10 July 1935, Lang Papers, Vol. 70, Lambeth Palace Library)."[1]

Many smaller groups, with the most sincere and worthy objectives, had proliferated, as well as some with less laudable aims, such as power or sensation seeking. Out of all this, many intelligent and cautious church members (ordained as well as lay) were coming to conclusions which they wanted to explore further, but were wishing to do so in the company of fellow Christians and within a framework which held its Christian beliefs to be of the first importance. More of this background will be explored in other chapters as appropriate, but from the foregoing it will be seen that the new "Fellowship" was not a mushroom growth but a fresh shoot from a root system which had been developing for a long time, until the conditions were suitable for it to appear in the light of day.

So, in due course, the Rev. F.S.W. Simpson ("a forthright and fearless speaker and writer who felt intensely the urgency for the study of the paranormal to be brought inside the Christian churches)"[2] was responsible for bringing together the two inspired and energetic persons who were to be the main movers in the founding and active life of what was to become the CFPSS.

Lieutenant Colonel Reginald Lester (soon to be known always as "Col. Lester" to Fellowship members) had been a soldier in both "the Great War" and the 1939-45 War. He had witnessed death in many horrifying forms (including the Battle of the Somme), and had not found traditional Christian belief or the clergy able to satisfy his many questions. Then he came to face his greatest test when his first wife died in 1948; and again he found no solace in the church in this his great personal bereavement. An experienced and prominent journalist, his work brought him into contact with Air Chief Marshal Lord Dowding, who persuaded him into psychic investigation, although

Reginald Lester was intensely sceptical about such a quest. However his investigations and discoveries caused him to change his mind drastically, and in an effort to help others he wrote his book: "In Search of the Hereafter".[3] As a result of the publication of this book he received 800 letters of support and enquiry, and this, remembering his own difficult search, imbued him with the idea that there was a great need for such an enquiry among Christian church members.

The Rev. Maurice Elliott, an Anglican clergyman, had spent the greater part of his life in the study of psychic science and its bearing on Scripture, Philosophy and Theology. Responsible for a great output of pamphlets and books, conducting a wide-ranging campaign, and speaking in support of other societies promoting the views to which he had become passionately devoted, always his purpose was to bring these truths, as he saw them, into the Christian church.

Both he and Reginald Lester were convinced that: "the gifts of the Holy Spirit in the Church, which is the 'blessed company of all faithful people', are meant to be permanent and exercised *today* (see Cor. I Chapter 12); and that 'seers' and 'sensitives' are with us *today* and that their gifts should be dedicated to the service of God and mankind." (Original Aims and Objects of the CFPS).[4]

They believed that the wave of psychic interest from Victorian times to date (and Maurice Elliott was one among many original Fellowship members who had been members of the Society for Psychical Research) was directed towards something in nature needing to be investigated as part of a scientific contribution towards a greater understanding of humanity. Maurice Elliott was also amongst many who believed that in this field there were spiritual implications in which all Christians should be vitally interested and involved, helping to combat the pervasive materialistic thinking which had developed from the so-called Ages of Reason and Enlightenment, and which was now so firmly established as the rightful and logical mind-set for the twentieth century.

For Maurice Elliott this life-long commitment had no doubt been influenced by the fact that his wife was a talented and natural Christian sensitive. For Reginald Lester it had arisen from a deep emotional and intellectual conversion, as a result of his bereavement and subsequent investigations into psychic phenomena, including mediumship, leading him into what was to become an idealistic crusade for the rest of his life.

Many other clergy and lay people had reached that point by similar paths, and at the right time the pattern had begun to weave. Many were drawn to devote time and energy to the new society, seeing it as serving a cause in which they believed wholeheartedly. In this short history it is not possible to give a full measure of recognition to all involved, but throughout the tracing of the founding and development of the Fellowship, and in connection with subjects covered in succeeding chapters, names will be mentioned whenever appropriate. Pamphlets, books, tapes, conference records, are available to any who might want to read further about the earlier days, the first members, their origins, words and thoughts.

Equally, it would make a cumbersome chapter to discuss at this stage the ramifications of conflicting and controversial issues of science, theology, healing, parapsychology, and the reactions and views of those more orthodox in their beliefs within the churches and therefore fearful of or opposed to these studies. These matters are of great importance, and they will be considered in the later chapters given to different aspects of the whole subject. However, even at this stage, when looking at the early founding members, it should always be remembered that their motives were utterly sincere and they followed the truth as they saw it.

So, then, at that first meeting in November, 1953, there came together: Col. Reginald Lester, the Rev. Maurice Elliott, the Rev. Charles Harrington, the Rev. Canon John Pearce-Higgins, the Rev. Canon W.S. Pakenham-Walsh, and the Rev. F.S. Simpson – five clergymen, all Anglican, and one layman, Col. Lester, later to become an Anglican reader.

The meeting was recorded in the form of Minutes, and it was apparent from the outset that matters were to be conducted in a business-like way, no doubt thanks to the organising ability and communications skills of Reginald Lester, described as "genius" by a later Chairman (now the President, the Rev. Dr Martin Israel). Membership was to be advertised by means of a letter to the press, including the statement of Aims and Objectives already quoted; and this letter, already prepared in draft form, was to be circulated to the committee for comment and amendment where desired. Before any public appeal, however, individual members of this first committee were to approach "people holding positions of some authority in the Churches who would be willing to lend their names to public support of this Fellowship". Names such as Dr W.R. Matthews, Dean of St. Paul's, Dr Leslie Weatherhead and Bishop Cuthbert Bardsley, were typical of those put forward, with all of those mentioned being known to one or other member of the committee. It was also decided that a Standing Committee should be set up with invitations going to members of orthodox Free Churches.

Reginald Lester was in the Chair at this meeting but was not elected officially as Chairman until later. Meanwhile, at the second meeting on Tuesday, December 5th, the title was changed to "the Churches' Fellowship for Psychical Study" and was to remain in that form for the next ten years. The draft public letter with the Aims and Objects was discussed and amended and finalised.

On 23rd February, 1954, at the third meeting of the founding committee a great deal was accomplished. Reginald Lester was formally elected as Chairman, with Maurice Elliott becoming Hon. Secretary/Treasurer. Sir Cyril Atkinson, a Judge of the High Court of Justice (King's Bench Division) from 1933 – 1948, member of Parliament from 1924 – 1933, and a member of the Church Assembly, had been approached and had agreed to become President, and was duly elected. Canon Pakenham-Walsh was elected Vice-President.

It was agreed that the open letter, with the Aims and Objects, should be sent to all national and major provincial daily and Sunday newspapers, and to the ecclesiastical press, on March 31st; and a draft was approved for a form letter to be sent to all resulting enquirers.[5] Estimates for printing headed notepaper were considered and one chosen; and the proofs of the Aims and Objects, which the Greater World Christian Spiritualist Church had kindly offered to print free of charge, were considered, but it was decided to ask for a better quality paper! Bankers and approved cheque signatories were appointed, and procedures outlined for committee members' expenses.

At subsequent committee meetings this efficient organisational work continued. In March 1954, the pattern of membership was established, with full membership open only to those who belonged to churches which were members of or affiliated to the World Council of Churches. Others would be welcomed, but only as associate members and therefore without the right to vote. Thus it was ensured that only Christian church members would have power to affect the running of the Fellowship.

Public awareness was considered, and it was agreed that the names of all principal supporters to date should be added to the heading of the next circular letter; and arrangements were to be made for a press cutting agency to be engaged. Policy for dealing with adverse comments in the press was agreed.

Mrs Gwen Vivian, who was already much engaged in Fellowship work, was invited to join the committee. Mrs Vivian, a Cambridge graduate who had studied psychic science for 18 years, and who had thus found consolation in the loss of a young daughter, was a lifelong Methodist and came from an old Methodist family. A little later Mrs Olive Field was to be asked to join the committee, her main interest lying in the healing ministry, assisting the Rev. D. Mercer Wilson in his healing services at St. George the Martyr's Church, London W.C.1, and serving on the committee of the Free Church Home of Divine Healing in Bournemouth.

In April plans were initiated for the first public meeting, to be held at Caxton Hall, Westminster; and this was to be advertised in all major church newspapers and in the psychic press. A special sub-committee to deal with this meeting was set up, and for the first time the name of Miss Alice White is mentioned. There is, so far, no record of her already doing voluntary secretarial work for the Fellowship, but this is obviously what had been happening, and in June she and a Mrs Compton were thanked for their work to date. Thus they were the first of a continuous stream of vital and largely unsung voluntary workers.

A London sub-committee, with the Rev. Vincent and Mrs Howson, and Mrs Olive Field, was set up to arrange for "drawing-room" and parish hall meetings. There was discussion about the choice of books to be recommended to members.

Committee meetings until now had been held at the Lesters'

flat, but in May, 1954, the committee meeting took place in the Deanery at St. Paul's, underlining the continuing support of the Dean, Dr W.R. Matthews. Maurice Elliott was able to announce that the membership already stood at 500.

In June Reginald Lester announced that Maurice Elliott (now 70 years of age) had resigned his living, in Chichester, in order to be able to devote himself full-time to the Fellowship. It was agreed that he should be paid a modest salary to compensate him to some extent. More names were put forward to serve on the monthly Standing Committee; and, to carry on with more urgent business, plans were made for the setting up of Executive, Research and Library Committees. The question of a quarterly bulletin was raised, and it was agreed that for the time being this should be a cyclo-styled one, with the Rev. F.W.S. Simpson, Maurice Elliott and Miss White responsible for its preparation.

The need for a London office was felt to be urgent, especially as many enquiries about healing were being received, and proper premises were obviously necessary for any serious work to be undertaken. Meanwhile the Chairman suggested that the Committee should undertake the work of absent (or prayer) healing, sharing the names amongst them. They were not to know but the London office would not be possible for another seven years.

Maurice Elliott spoke of his anxiety that the study groups should be under the leadership of Christian full members of the Fellowship; and that meetings should be opened with prayer, and with studies directed towards suitable passages from the New Testament. Here was the development of one of the most important strands of Fellowship work (as opposed to mainly organisational matters); and this, together with the question of policy on mediumship (deferred from May) was to be something requiring much thought and care in the months and years to come, as will be seen in the following chapters. Finally plans were discussed for the next public meeting at Caxton Hall, and for four other smaller meetings, three in London and one in Leicester.

In July two other important committee meetings took place. The first was of the full Standing Committee, now large enough to necessitate moving to the vestry at St. Mary's Church, Putney, the church of Canon John Pearce-Higgins. One important matter had to be dealt with, altering arrangements made at the last meeting. Maurice Elliott reported that the volume of clerical and secretarial work had increased to such an extent that it was overwhelming the two voluntary part-time helpers, Mrs Compton and Miss Alice White. He therefore proposed that he should revert to being honorary Secretary/Treasurer, thus releasing the salary proposed for him; and that Miss White, who was agreeable, should give up her other employment and become a full-time employee of the Fellowship for the same salary. This was agreed, and Miss Alice White was duly appointed as Assistant Secretary, a position which she was to hold with efficiency and dedication for a great many years.

There was also held on the same day the first meeting of the Executive Committee, and the two committees initiated or confirmed business and policies which were to be important for the future years. Matters such as healing, mediumship and research will be discussed in the relevant chapters; but here let it be noted that Mrs Grace Lester (Reginald's second wife) was invited to serve on the newly appointed Healing Committee, thus entering the records of the Fellowship for the first time, at the beginning of her many years of devoted service to the cause. Other significant names were mentioned. Mr Brodie Lodge, son of Sir Oliver, was elected to the Standing Committee, as were the Rev. Selwyn Roberts and Canon Carpenter. There were reports of favourable and adverse comments in the press, and steps were agreed to deal with both.

In September, 1954 the first issue of the "News Sheet" appeared, a modest 4-page printed leaflet, containing mostly factual information about meetings and committee work to date. This was to be issued quarterly until December, 1957, when it would have grown to 12 pages, including articles and much news of regional affairs, now countrywide. The next issue, March 1958, took the new title of "Quarterly Review", with 14 pages and a newly designed cover in blue and white, and a picture incorporating the cross over the world, with supporting angels holding an open book with the inscription "concerning spiritual gifts". The new title, "Quarterly Review", with changes of format from time to time, has remained in force until today, the journal itself continuing to be the central link for members all over the country and abroad.

So, in September, 1954, with the first issue of a journal, the membership now at 1,000, and various projects initiated for different committees to handle, a sound framework was being established. The main protagonists in this beginning now embarked on a decade of enthusiastic promotion and consolidation of the work so well begun.

During this time the majority of those involved were still working at their various professions. Reginald Lester was a full-time journalist, and in 1956 was elected President of the Institute of Journalists, which office he combined with his promotion of the Fellowship, for instance during his visit to Scandinavia. His book "In Search of the Hereafter" was selling in countries such as the U.S.A., Japan and Sweden, and all enquirers were referred to the Fellowship. The clergy members still served in their various church appointments, sometimes finding the time spent in this dual interest costing them dearly, as when Canon John Pearce-Higgins, by then Vice-Provost of Southwark, had to resign from that position.

However, at whatever cost, the work went on, with a formal constitution being drawn up in 1956, with amendments in 1960. Branches were being set up all over the country, and in 1957 the system of regions was organised, thus bringing in one of the most valuable contributions to the Fellowship's continuing strength. There were "At Homes", and other social functions, church services, and a clergy conference, most enthusiastically received. The importance to members of seeing authoritative names as part of the official structure was always firmly in the forefront of Maurice Elliott's and Reginald Lester's thinking. Issue No. 11 (December, 1956) of the "News Sheet" was the first issue to carry a list of honorary Vice Presidents, 26 in all, of which half were clergy (including four Bishops, one dean and five canons). The lay list was a roll call of titles and distinguished names, undoubtedly all sincerely interested in the Fellowship's work.

For the first years office accommodation was provided through the goodwill and generosity of members, first in London, then for two years in Hove, and then in Worthing, from 1956 – 1961. Then in 1961 finally the long-held hope was achieved, and suitable offices were rented at Denison House, near Victoria Station, the first real "Headquarters", and to be the centre of the work for many years.

During this time all the leading members travelled around the country speaking to large and small public meetings and Fellowship branches and groups. During the period March to July 1962, for example, Reginald and Grace Lester attended 13 groups or public meetings from the south to the north of England; and it was in this period undoubtedly that Grace Lester became the well-loved friend and sympathetic listener to so many who found much consolation and healing in her gentle company and profound faith.

A firm control over standards was maintained, in the often repeated emphasis on the need for study, with all levels, physical, mental and spiritual "in their right perspective", in the words of the Rev. Dr John McDonald, a tireless organiser of study groups. By December 1957, there were 10 to his credit in Leeds alone, reflecting his own brilliant career as theologian, scientist and expert in semitic languages. On this occasion, however, he was speaking as the first Maurice Elliott Memorial Lecturer, at Caxton Hall in September, 1960. For Maurice Elliott, that great crusader and pioneer, had died in June 1959, at the age of 75. The loss felt by the Fellowship is demonstrated in the many tributes printed in the journals, and at the memorial service held at St. Martin's-in-the-Fields in October. He was, as Reginald Lester said in the first obituary, "a man of courage and dedication who felt that his lifelong aim had come to pass with the founding of the Fellowship." [7]

There is no doubt that he had suffered much for his uncompromising and determined work to bring the field of psychical studies within the Christian church; but, as it was said, never was there any rancour or bitterness in his outlook; and all who knew him spoke of his loving wisdom. He forthrightly condemned what he saw to be the caricatures of the truth often to be found in much of spiritualism, while paying tribute to the integrity and worth of much of the work accomplished. This must be considered in greater depth in the appropriate chapter. [8]

Meanwhile another devoted worker had taken Maurice Elliott's place as Honorary Secretary. This was the Rev. Bertram Woods, a retired Methodist minister who had already served on many of the committees before taking on the rôle of

Secretary, which he was to hold for many years. His main concern was and remained in the field of healing and he combined this with his Secretary's duties with great effectiveness.[9]

Continuing concern to emphasise the spiritual content of Fellowship studies came to a head in March, 1963, when a referendum was held to decide on the question of a change of title to make that concern apparent. This was in response to the proposal submitted to the previous Annual General Meeting by Miss Frances Banks, who had begun and was to continue to make a great contribution to the Fellowship's studies in prayer and mysticism. As a result of that referendum, in which a decisive majority voted for the new title, the society became The Churches' Fellowship for Psychical and Spiritual Studies.

In the same issue of the journal in which this was reported[10] there appeared a message from the Archbishop of Canterbury, the Most Rev. Michael Ramsey, through his Senior Chaplain, the Rev. N.M. Kennaby, which read: "His Grace is anxious that the Fellowship for Psychical Study should be a body such as would commend itself to the Church and command the confidence of church people in the important work which it is carrying out. In saying this, I do not mean to imply that this is not already the case. It is, however, for this reason that the Archbishop would be very happy to help in the appointment of a President to succeed Sir Cyril Atkinson."

By now the number of Bishops among the Patrons (the new designation, replacing that of Hon. Vice President) had risen to 22, plus the Archbishop of Wales. Therefore, on the departure of Sir Cyril Atkinson, it seemed most suitable that the new President should combine both legal and ecclesiastical weight. Such a man was the Worshipful Chancellor the Rev. E. Garth Moore, M.A., J.P., and Chancellor of three dioceses. At that time he held many lectureships and legal appointments, and was President of the Cambridge Psychical Research Society, and a member of the Society for Psychical Research. Thus the Fellowship was privileged to have a remarkably qualified and gifted man to guide it through the next 20 years.

Now the work was to grow in many ways. There would be difficulties as well as successes; and certainly the task undertaken was never to be simple. Prejudice and opposition (from spiritualists as well as churches) were to be met, as well as recognition and encouragement. In all these endeavours many faithful members, whose names perhaps will never be mentioned, worked devotedly. To see how the work has developed to date it is simpler now to change from chronological narrative to consideration of the different aspects of the studies undertaken; and in Chapter 3 it is necessary to look at the originally central and most controversial part of the work of the CFPSS.

CHAPTER 3

The CFPSS and the Hereafter

Almost as soon as it was founded, the work of the (then) Churches' Fellowship for Psychical Study began to broaden to bring in other subjects of concern to Christians, such as healing, prayer, meditation and mysticism; but there is no doubt that the founding members had had their thoughts specifically directed to the lack of teaching and understanding, as they saw it, within the Christian church with regard to the "last things", with special reference to the destination and condition of the departed soul or spirit. As has already been touched upon, this concern arose from the great void in this area felt by many Christians from the Reformation onwards, increasing in the eighteenth and nineteenth centuries with the growing influences of the materialistic sciences.

This sense of deprivation rose to its greatest height (or sank to its lowest depth) during and after the Great or First World War, agonisingly exacerbated by horrifying casualties. For example, it is hard to comprehend the effect on the nation of the loss in 1916 of 500,000 of its young men in one three-month campaign, the Somme, this figure alone being equal to the sum total of deaths, British, Commonwealth and civilian, in the whole of the 1939-45 War. As it was, the four years of war, 1914-1918, with its millions of deaths, was followed by a plague, the so-called 'Spanish influenza', which swept Europe, causing millions more deaths in the already weakened civilian populations, food deprivation having been far worse than it was, for instance, permitted to be in the second world war.

Thus, in the 1920s and 1930s, battling with anguish and doubts, people sought consolation and answers within the Churches, and, it has to be said, failed to be satisfied with what they found in the Anglican/Protestant churches. The founders of the Fellowship had lived through both world wars and could not have felt more deeply the need for their churches to be true sources of faith and comfort. Yet Canon John Pearce-Higgins could say, as late as 1966: "When our leading thinkers, who seem to be so wrapped up in problems of demythologisation and the secular meaning of the gospel, are apparently quite unable to grapple with the problem of the hereafter, it is little wonder that the rank and file of the clergy, with exceptions, fall down on this job. I have, when opportunity offered, questioned leading theologians, from Bishop Robinson downwards, over the problems of survival, who all gave me the same reply. 'The Christian faith is not concerned with survival, it is concerned with eternal life'. If I reply that surely survival is a pre-condition of eternal life, they sidestep by talking about the quality of life and our relationship with God being the important thing. No doubt this is true, but it does not appear to be relevant at the parochial level of the ordinary man and woman who want to know after a funeral whether they will meet their loved one again and in what sort of condition."[1]

Theology is a living science, and therefore the relationship between it and the churches' teachings always has and always will be in a fluid state; and there have been and inevitably will be different reactions from different parts of the Christian church as a whole. To quote just two examples: On February 3rd, 1984 in the "Church Times" Bishop Cyril Eastaugh, writing as President of the Guild of All Souls, found it extraordinary that a priest should ask: "Why pray for the dead?" Yet the fact that the priest had indeed asked that question demonstrated the wide divergency of views held. In 1991, in their book: "Requiem Healing", the authors, Michael Mitton and Russ Parker, showed very clearly how they were moving from the accepted Evangelical view, that the subject of "the dead" was dangerous and barred, to a situation of "giving people permission to love their dead".[2]

It is obvious, therefore, from the beginnings of the Fellowship that it was undertaking work in an area of great difficulty, wherein lay wide differences between the varying theologies held within the body of the Christian church, these differences reflecting the scepticism or indifference of contemporary culture.

How had this come about? Most cultures or belief systems provide a background affording a relationship with their peoples' ancestors, thus creating an outlet for grief and a continuing therapeutic view of the place of the individual in the scheme of things, both here and hereafter, and thus a sense of security in an otherwise neutral and daunting universe. The Chinese, the Greeks, the Hindus, the Jews, and other great religions, and uncountable sub-cultures, all have or had their beliefs and understanding of the ancestors, spirits, heroes, gods, messengers, who inhabited that other dimension we move into at death, and which could be acknowledged reverently and naturally.

In early and mediaeval Christianity the Resurrection of Christ and teachings of the place of the departed in Christ, together with the rôle of Mary and all the saints, and the practice of prayers for the departed, kept this necessary life and death perspective in balance; and ordinary people had a death-embracing faith and culture arising from that faith. Unfortunately with familiarity comes not only contempt but corruption; so much so that it could be said of mediaeval faith: "In monasteries, largely under the influences of Cluny, it became the rule to say the Offices of the Dead daily. It would be difficult to exaggerate the degree to which the whole of later mediaeval worship was dominated by the thought of the departed, and particularly for the need for shortening the pains of purgatory. This excessive domination to some extent explains the violent reaction of the Reformation against prayers for the departed altogether ... The lack of any clear Scriptural sanction for prayers for the departed caused Cranmer to reduce them to the very minimum. This defect, for such it is now felt to be by most students who attempt to achieve a balanced view of Christian teaching, assisted to widen the chasm between the living and the dead."[3]

The post-Reformation funeral service of the 1662 Prayer Book, that book held to be of "extraordinary beauty, serving the Church of England for three hundred years", is "clearly directed at the living and not the dead."[4] So, in the 1960s the Church of England Liturgical Commission came to work on a new funeral service, meeting the need for more positive joy (as with the services of the Early Church), and alternatives for crematoria, the death of a child, and the growing pressure from Anglo-Catholics for prayers for the dead and for funeral Eucharists. Parallel changes (or opposition to change) can no doubt be traced in the Reformed and Free churches.

In all of this, from its foundation in 1953, the CFPSS sought always to make a worthwhile contribution, based on the Christian faith, Scriptural sources, and a new study of the experiences and insights of sensitives within the Fellowship, or, if not members, then of recognised integrity.

In 1939 the Lang commission on Spiritualism had completed its report (as already mentioned in Chapter 2, and see also Chapter 5). For a brief summary of the vicissitudes of that report a "Christian Parapsychologist" editorial by the Ven. Michael Perry is very useful. For various good reasons his concluding words are: "Can we now bury it and, instead, let the CFPSS alert the Christian world to the importance of the psychic dimension to human experience, and the need for it to be integrated within orthodox Christian theology, spirituality and practice?"[5]
In 1991 that must seem the best way in which to go forward, but when studying the history of the Fellowship there is no doubt that the clergy founding members were, in 1953, pioneering a Christian approach to psychic studies which was for them painful and difficult, and for which the need was highlighted by the terms of reference of the Underhill Report, and the lack of success of that commission in making a case sufficient to influence two Bishops' meetings. This is the more to be deplored when one re-reads the text, in the journal "Light", of the talk given at the College of Psychic Studies by Father Geoffrey Curtis, CR, that wise and loving monk, in which he gently deprecates the theological snobbery which had influenced the dissenting minority on the commission; also the lack of reference to the need for pastoral care (now so much a part of the Anglican ministry of deliverance). However, he ends with the quotation from the Report which perhaps best illustrates the CFPSS current attitude to the study of things psychic and the continuing life of the human spirit: "the recognition of the nearness of our friends who have died, and of their progress in the spiritual life, and of their continuing concern for us, cannot do otherwise, for those who have experienced it, than add a new immediacy and richness to their

belief in the Communion of Saints."[6]

This could well express the founding impetus of the CFPSS, and still remains one of its policy views today. To deny the validity and the relevance of the experiences and developing beliefs of Christian sensitives is to deny that important part of Christian witness, the gift of discernment of spirits, as given by St. Paul in I Cor. 12. Whether it be a vivid awareness of the ministry of angels (as with Maurice Elliott's wife Irene), or visions and openness to saints and teachers, or an ability to attune to the ordinary discarnate soul with a need to be dealt with, or with a mission of love to family on earth, these witnesses are described in so many books and booklets published by or through the work of the CFPSS; and it can indeed be seen that a renewed faith in the Communion of Saints and the ministry of angels has been the result for many.[7]

Fellowship writers and scholars have always striven to work within the boundaries of the Scriptures and Christian doctrine. For instance, in the booklet version of the Fourth Maurice Elliott Memorial Lecture (published in 1964), called "The Christian Doctrine of the Hereafter in the Light of Psychical Research", the Rev. Bertram Woods, then a retired Methodist Minister and Honorary Secretary of the Fellowship, dealt with the question of orthodox doctrine, Gospel teachings and what the "new" study of psychic sources could contribute to a developing theology. He also drew attention to the painstaking work of Robert Crookall, who in "The Supreme Adventure" collated so much testimony, including a great deal from doctors, nurses and sensitives, which would, he hoped, appeal to those outside the Church but prepared to look at evidence supporting Scriptural teachings.[8]

This work has been continued in numerous Fellowship publications over the years. For example booklets such as the Rev. Dr Martin Israel's "The Life of the World to Come" and "The Intermediate Dimension"; the Ven. Michael Perry's "The Spiritual Implications of Survival"; and the Fellowship book "Life, Death and Psychical Research" (published in 1973) which brought together much of the thinking and conclusions, at that time, of many valuable contributors. Helen Greaves, a notable Fellowship sensitive, wrote several books, the most outstanding of which "Testimony of Light", inspired by the deceased

Frances Banks, continues to be reprinted and provide inspiration and comfort.[9] In lectures, and articles in the Fellowship's own journals and in other religious publications the work continues, with contributions from scholars and those who are willing to describe their own spiritual experiences.

The importance of such work, beyond the need of the individual, is perhaps best expressed by Bishop Morris Maddocks in his book "The Christian Healing Ministry". He says: "Much of our depression and stress emanate from an unsatisfactory relationship with those who have gone before us. For our health it should be brought out into the openness of Christ, and the Eucharist is both the time and place for this healing to be received:" and: "We are storing up for ourselves epidemics of dis-ease unless we are healed into a right relationship with our dead. Only the transfiguring radiance of the presence of Jesus can heal this wound of separation."[10]

In 1963, in his first Presidential address, Chancellor Garth Moore said: "Psychical research, like all creation, tells us something of the Creator; and it is proper for man to look upon all creation and therefrom to learn more of the Creator. It is within that motive and in that spirit that I, for my part, should like to think that this Fellowship will continue to pursue the studies to which it is dedicated."[11] In 1983, in his last Presidential letter, he continued that same theme, that psychic phenomena are part of Creation, and all creation is worth studying because it provides a clue to the mind of the Creator, saying: "Christian theology (and indeed all theology and also the natural sciences) should take account of the paranormal ... it is strange indeed that Christians, who rely so heavily on the Biblical accounts of the miraculous, should be so slow to welcome evidence which goes so far to destroy the assertions of their opponents that such things never occurred because they are intrinsically impossible."[12]

In a letter, written in 1991, telling of his memories of the 1953 founding of the CFPSS, the Rev. Selwyn Roberts said of those days: "The average pew sitter had little conviction about life after death, and the silence of clergy so often bewildered the folk who had lost loved ones, and others who had intimations of spirituality of the heavenly kind." In an article in the "Church Times" on 18th January 1991, concerning the move of the Rev. Dr William Oddie from the Anglican to the Roman Catholic church, he (Dr Oddie) is quoted as saying that "a high percentage of Anglican clergy have no belief in life after death."

It might appear, therefore, that little progress has been made between 1953 and 1991, but this is a short span of time in the history of the faith. CFPSS members, clergy and lay, are aware that the life of the Fellowship takes place within the climate of our era, through the post-war despair of the 20s and 30s, the disillusion of the war-time 40s and the following 50s, the secular theology of the 60s, the occult explosion of the 70s, and the brash success-dominated society and New Age beliefs of the 80s. Theology and spirituality need scholarship, wisdom and discernment. The work goes on, and includes many other areas of Christian experience, as will be seen in the following chapters.

CHAPTER 4

The CFPSS and the Ministry of Healing

"During the first three hundred years of its history the Church continued its proclamation of the risen Lord through its preaching and healing."[1] I am quoting again from Morris Maddocks' "The Christian Healing Ministry", and would like to quote more but I can only suggest that interested readers would find therein a useful account of healing within the Christian Church from its first days to date. It is certainly clear that when the Church moved from the era of persecution to that of acceptance it became more concerned with organisation and theology rather than with spiritual practice, so that gradually the possibility of healing in this world became the theory of salvation in the next. "This process has been reversed in the Latin Church only as recently as 1962, when the anointing with oil was reinstated as a sacrament of healing."[2]

So, although during the mediaeval period the care and cure of the sick and pilgrims was the work of many of the monastic orders, during the 1,700 years from the third century until the present, healing as a manifestation of the divine was comparatively rarely heard of or practised. In this century, however, a great revival in the study and application of the Church's healing ministry has taken place, through the work of greatly gifted individuals (for instance Hickson, Kerin, Bennett, Weatherhead), and the inspiration and leadership of archbishops (notably Temple, Ramsey and Coggan) through various Lambeth Conferences from 1908 to 1978. In later years the nonconformist churches (Methodist, United Reformed and Baptist) have also set up their own systems of healing. However, despite all this, developments have been too slow for those longing to see the work grow, and certainly in 1953, when the CFPSS was founded, healing services, conferences and societies were by no means the norm as seen in the churches today.

Outside the churches much else had been happening. In the last century the great inflow of the spirit which led to the spiritualist movement and the setting up of the Society for Psychical Research and other similar bodies seemed to be the opening for the renewed entry of healing energy into the world, although the source of that energy was and is much disputed. At the same time, gradually, a more would-be scientific approach to non-medical healing was growing, culminating in the many-faceted array of complementary medicines and therapies now available, with, in this area too, disputed esoteric systems and theories complicating the overall picture.

Into this no-man's land, between church and unorthodox spiritual or spiritist practice, the newly-fledged Churches' Fellowship for Psychical Study (as it then was) raised its unwary head, and was nearly overwhelmed or taken over. However, sound leadership brought it through into a well-founded position, such testing times occurring most notably at its inception and once again much later in its history. Perhaps these crises were inevitable. The Fellowship, in the bridging rôle already mentioned in Chapter 1, provides a forum for members belonging to other organisations concerned with healing, ranging from the orthodox to the universalist, thus forming sometimes comfortable, often uncomfortable links with mutually disapproving factions. As will be seen, the leadership tended more and more towards the orthodox, but always there was a minority of members of different inspiration and gifts choosing to work independently or with organisations outside the orthodox fold, while remaining true as they saw it to their allegiance to the main Christian church. These tensions continue, and perhaps serve a valuable purpose. As one encouraging bishop put it: "The Church needs pressure groups; and in any case independent, sincere 'dissenters' are safer with you than completely outside the church".

To go back to the beginning. With the first committee meeting having been held only on 10th November, 1953, at the meeting on 30th June 1954, "The Chairman raised the matter of healing, and reported that every week members were writing in to enquire what part healing was going to take in the Fellowship's activities." He also reported that many others were asking for 'absent healing' and it was agreed that something had to be done in response to these appeals. On July 20th the matter was discussed further. By then nearly 200 requests for 'absent healing' had been received. It was agreed that such requests must be dealt with in a proper way, and for the time being the names would be divided between committee members, but a special healing committee would need to be set up.

There had been some favourable reporting, in the "Daily Mail", for instance, but the "Daily Herald" appeared to have got things wrong. Col. Lester, with his journalistic background, saw the demand for healing as a great opportunity for the Fellowship to move forward, but there is no doubt that in general the Committee recognised the great responsibility and deeper implications of such requests. The first meeting of the Committee on Healing took place on 4th August, 1954. Here such matters as recording methods and proper preparation of 'patients' were settled; and overall the importance of prayer as the basis for all healing work and the submission of individual needs to God's will. A further meeting on 18th August was necessary to settle other matters of organisation and practice.

It was at this meeting that the use of the term 'absent healing' was queried in a letter from Canon Pearce-Higgins which was read to the committee; but his objection and request for the words 'intercession' and 'intercessors' to be substituted was not accepted. However, at the Standing Committee meeting on 9th September 1954, all the clergy members expressed doubt at the use of the word 'healer'. Maurice Elliott questioned the validity of the instructions sent by the healing committee to 'patients', and read a letter from the Dean of St. Paul's (Dr W.R. Matthews) in which he expressed his apprehension about this same matter. He also thought that the Fellowship would be wise to wait until the contemporary Archbishops' Commission on Divine Healing, of which Maurice Elliott was a member, had completed its studies. (The Commission reported in 1958, and Maurice Elliott had to dissociate himself from what it said about spiritualism). It was eventually agreed that the Rev. Selwyn Roberts, already on the Standing and Executive Committees, and a member of the (then) Churches' Council for Healing, should join the Fellowship healing committee. Finally, Col.

Lester mentioned that the Press had received misleading statements about the Fellowship's work from other sources, and it was agreed that only official statements should be issued at intervals.

Meanwhile the greatest minefield had still to be negotiated – in the area of mediumship, thought to be a legitimate subject for study, and its overlap with the gift of healing which many sensitives undoubtedly had. Here again the problem of 'the dead', Scriptural prohibitions, and modern interpretations had to be taken into account. In his booklet "Many Avenues" (now out of print) the Rev. Bertram Woods listed under "Prayer Therapy" three methods: "True Prayer – communion with God; Meditation – focussed health-giving thoughts; and Absent Healing – by which we contact helpers in the realm of Spirit." Not everyone who was doing the work of 'absent healing' would have accepted that last definition.

Later, in 1977, Chancellor Garth Moore (by then President) in his booklet "The Church's Ministry of Healing" was to say: "The Christian believes in the Communion of Saints, which means the communion of all Christians, living and departed. All that we know is that when healing is effected the only true healer is God." The matter remains controversial, and not all Fellowship members hold to one view. The one common belief is, in the words of Dorothy Kerin, an early member, that the work of the Christian is to help in healing the sick, comforting the sorrowing, and restoring faith to the faithless.

So, back in the 1950s, the committee of the Fellowship continued to encourage and monitor the fast-growing healing side of the work, the clergy trying to keep within the limits of current church theology and practice, and the medical members seeking the co-operation of the BMA and individual doctors.

For many years there was a strong input from members of the medical profession, an outstanding example being Dr Griffith Evans, FRCS, who combined his medical skills with an interest in modern physics and a dedication to the cause of spiritual healing and the reconciling of healing with science. He gave ten years of work to Fellowship committees, conferences and journals.[3] Other medically qualified members gave outstanding support, such as Dr W.S. Ford Robertson who equalled Dr Griffith Evans in his kindness and unobtrusive help to individuals.

In 1964 Dr Michael Ash pioneered experiments into the chemical changes of water and other substances in contact with those with healing gifts; and in 1969 a note in the June issue of the "Quarterly Review" reported the formation of a CFPSS Medical Section under the Rev. Dr Kenneth Cuming as a result of consultations with the Institute of Religion and Medicine, from which it was hoped would develop closer co-operation between the Fellowship and the medical profession. Although a great deal of thought and time was given to inter-disciplinary meetings, not much was heard from this committee, and eventually many medical members of the Fellowship tended to be drawn to work with the Scientific and Medical Network (see also Chapter 5).

At the same time the Fellowship's early notice of the relationship between mental illness and some forms of possession or influences from non-human levels, developed naturally into interest and some expertise in the field of exorcism and deliverance. The natural gifts and medical qualifications of the Rev. Dr Martin Israel (by then Chairman of the Fellowship and President of the Guild of Health), resulted in his becoming a respected authority on these subjects, able to give wise and helpful guidance to Fellowship members as necessary. The late Rev. Alun Virgin, then a Council member, worked for many years with the Christian Exorcism Study Group (now the Christian Deliverance Study Group); and later the Ven. Michael Perry, currently Chairman of the CFPSS, acted as Editor in the production of the Christian Deliverance Study Group handbook "Deliverance" which is widely used by clergy dealing with psychic problems.[4] Over the years many clergy and lay members of the Fellowship have co-operated with the authorities or worked privately in dealing with problems in this complicated area.[5]

Throughout all these years the majority of members continued to work quietly in the ministry of healing, through their support of church services or prayer groups, learning to value the practice of meditation in healing work, and encouraged by articles in the "Quarterly Review" and speakers at meetings and conferences, both from the church and from more unorthodox or esoteric societies. The terms 'healer', 'contact healing', and 'absent healing' continued to be used, although with the growth of the charismatic healing movement within the Church 'laying-on-of-hands' became more general. Outstanding and gifted exponents, such as Dorothy Kerin, Linda Martel, Brother Mandus, were followed; and the phenomena of Wesley[6], Lourdes, Fatima and Padre Pio[7] studied.

As early as 1962 a report was published, prepared by the Healing Committee of the CFPSS and based on questionnaires collected in the three previous years, which came to the very sober conclusion that "a vast amount of spiritual healing is being practised today, some of it very unenlightened, though sincerely done. Very little is known of its processes and laws, but the committee is convinced that it is governed by laws and will one day be studied and applied scientifically."[8] This same report also emphasised that there was a unanimity that the power came from God and is not within the 'healer'. Certainly over the years healing work within the Fellowship has tended to be based on Christian prayer and services, and the more recent concept of counselling has become an important part of the work, both in bereavement and deliverance.

The Rev. Dr Martin Israel, Chairman and then President (1975 to date) has been an inspired leader in this work, through his numerous books, articles in the Fellowship journals, and unstinting addresses at meetings and conferences, his qualifications in medicine and theology making him a respected authority in church and medical circles, where the introduction of the numinous, even into the work of healing, might otherwise still be viewed with suspicion!

All this is an area in which the CFPSS still has a rôle, bridging the gaps between so many different agencies. Many years ago Maurice Frost, then General Secretary, and Martin Israel as Chairman wrote in the "Quarterly Review" complementary articles about sacramental and charismatic healing, and the rôle of the Communion of Saints through the Holy Spirit.[9] The work has continued since then and many others, too many to name, have made valuable contributions, in writing (see CFPSS book lists), speaking and ministering; but the principles underlying the guidelines mentioned above remain for present and future work.

CHAPTER 5

The CFPSS and Psychical Research

The term 'psychical research' covers a multitude of theories and prejudices (if not sins). One comparatively new theory, frequently expounded by Rhea White[1], is that in any psychical research the experimenter or observer will inevitably be involved, even affecting the outcome of the experiment. This is obviously very possible in any subjectively received or perceived material, and equally could be seen to play a part in any creative or evaluative type of work. However, believers in objectivity may be a little hard to persuade.

Whether subjectively or objectively, the CFPSS was committed to psychical research from its earliest days, a committee having been set up for that purpose at the Council meeting of 19th September, 1954. Canon John Pearce-Higgins was to lead the newly formed committee, which was in the first place to study the phenomena of mediumship, following in the wake of the long-established and respected Society for Psychical Research, to which many Fellowship members already belonged. The research committee was to have members with scientific, medical or theological qualifications, and Mrs Gwen Vivian, Dr Laurence and Mrs Phoebe Bendit were among the first to be invited. John Pearce-Higgins felt that the aim should be towards study rather than experimentation, and at a meeting held on 3rd November, 1954 he stressed that "the first thing is to get a theological basis for what we are doing." Hence, immediately a bias was introduced which was understandably felt to be necessary, for a church-based society, but which would lead to accusations of prejudice and of being controlled by the ecclesiastical hierarchy, although this question was not to come to a head for another 20 years. In contrast, the Society for Psychical Research took as its aim the completely unprejudiced, neutral view, to such an extent that it could be argued that much subjective (but none the less valid) material was ruled out. Equally the deeply committed and serious spiritualists were to feel that their work never received the recognition it should have because of traditional religious prejudice. (On this subject a continuing, never resolved battle of words was conducted between Col. Lester and Maurice Barbanell of the "Psychic News" in the columns of that paper and other journals and newspapers).[2]

As far as the church was concerned it was thought, by some but by no means all, just acceptable to visit a medium for research purposes, but not if there was a genuine emotional need. It would be a unique person without an emotional tie of some kind with someone who has died, and so this must raise the question: can any 'sitting', however experimental, be truly without some input from the allegedly neutral experimenter or investigator; and how can anyone judge the amount of negativity in the neutral attitude which might well impair the sensitivity of the subject and thus detract from the validity of the experiment? Of course there is never any shortage of spontaneously received material, some, as will be seen, very convincing, but none the less always open to the criticism of being either wish-fulfilment or anecdotal.

Setting off blithely yet earnestly across all these minefields the newly formed committee for psychical research began its work, covering a wide range of subjects and producing in the "News Sheet", later the "Quarterly Review", a wealth of articles and reports, varied, complex and skilfully argued, scientifically, medically or theologically. A recurring theme was the value of psychical research to the church, the subject of a talk by Dr Matthews, the Dean of St. Paul's, on BBC radio, arranged by Col. Lester.[3] Paranormal matters of all kinds were studied, such as radionic therapy, graphology, the effect of prayer on plant growth, UFOs, Kirlian and psychic photography, Raudive voices, psi in US and USSR defence research, and medical work such as mentioned in Chapter 4.

Such outstanding thinkers as Robert Crookall (see Chapter 3) and Dr Raynor Johnson, the physicist, wrote and lectured and were eagerly supported, always with the aim of helping those unable to accept a religious and spiritual world view because of the inroads of science. So Dr Raynor Johnson was quoted as saying that psychical research "is an encouragement to intelligent people not to regard miracles as a stumbling block to religion",[4] and in an article on "The Philosophical Implications of Psychical Research" John Pearce-Higgins wrote: "psychical research cannot do the work of religion, nor of theology either, but in our day and generation (if I am right) it *is* the ally of religion."[5]

During the years the view was always stoutly adhered to that despite its disagreeable (for some) connotations the word 'psychical' could not be abandoned because it contained the element of soul which the CFPSS founders and members held to be the core of the work. Thus other words, such as 'paranormal' could never be acceptable substitutes. A sub-committee was set up to study the spiritual and theological implications of all this, comprising John Pearce-Higgins, Frances Banks (that remarkable woman will be given more space in Chapter 6) and Donald Bretherton, who was to do so much valuable work in this field in the years to come.

This pattern was to continue for ten years, with a balance being held between studying the spiritual implications of the results of psychical research and, as far as possible, a neutral study of phenomena. Fresh examples of communication were examined, for instance the Grace Rosher direct writing in combination with expert graphological opinion; or historical classics, for example the Palm Sunday correspondences, were considered. All forms of mediumship were observed, with ESP and telepathy, together with a great deal of literature from other societies, independent authors and so on.

In 1964 the Committee was renamed the Central Committee for the Study of Psychical Phenomena, with John Pearce-Higgins and the Rev. Allan Barham continuing as Chairman and Secretary. At the same time a new committee was established for Scientific Research under the Chairmanship of Dr Griffith Evans. These two committees, focussing the work of many gifted and highly qualified thinkers, continued for another thirteen years to produce a volume of work, some based on membership participation in experiments with questionnaire collation,[6] and much on the fruits of observation and consideration, of which the following can only be a small sample.

"An Acceptable Basic Science for Psychical and Spiritual Studies" – the Rev. W.T. Wilkins, B.Sc.: "Pentecost and the Significance of Psychical Phenomena" – H.V. Bearman: "The Theological Implications of Psychical Research" – E. Garth Moore: "The Effect on Humanity of Knowledge of the After Life" – G. Blaker: "From Imagination to Reality by Analogies in Science" – Wilfred L. Shaw.[7]

In 1973, thanks to the work of members of the Psychical Research and Scientific committees, the Fellowship published "Life, Death and Psychical Research", edited by Canon John Pearce-Higgins and the Rev. G.W. Whitby, assisted by the Rev. Allan Barham and Mrs E. Percival. With a list of distinguished contributors, most but not all members of the Fellowship, this book has remained a useful resource, although of course research and theoretical development have moved on considerably in many aspects since those days.[8] A worthy successor is a looked-for product of the 90s.

In the early 70s there was a gradual shift of emphasis in the work. Canon Andrew Glazewski, a Polish Roman Catholic, chaplain of the Polish refugee settlement near Newton Abbot, will be remembered by many older members for his brilliant lectures, and for his quirky humour. "Think of a glass of whisky" he used to say to those who could not remember or pronounce his name. He was ahead of his time in many ways, one example being his use, in the 60s, of acupressure, based on acupuncture, as a resource for an intuitive healer. Over the years he shared his vision of a fusing of the spiritual, scientific and medical fields. Pursuing that vision he brought together other like-minded and far-sighted professional men and women, and out of those meetings gradually evolved the Scientific and Medical Network. This society, beginning life as an informal and occasional meeting of interested academics, developed into an organisation which attracted those who felt freer outside a traditional theological framework.

At the same time the Fellowship was moving into the concept of Christian parapsychology, and in fact the journal of that title first saw the light in September, 1975 (see Chapter 8). At this same time, (in 1977) the Council thought it best, for various reasons, to suspend Fellowship committees, with a view to later reconstitution. This encouraged the tendency of scientifically or medically trained members, especially those already unable to accept the necessity to work within traditional theological patterns, to devote more time to the Scientific and Medical Network and other societies and projects.

It is impossible to evaluate the effect or influence of the great volume of work which had been accomplished over the 23 years since the first setting up of the Psychical Research committee in 1954. Even to pay a fitting tribute to the dedicated work of those who gave so much of their time, energy and devotion is not easy. Gratitude and appreciation, as expressed in the journals for John Pearce-Higgins, Allan Barham and H.V. Bearman, convey some idea, but they themselves would only want to be seen to be representative of the work done by so many others.[9]

All the while, individual contributors generously shared their own experiences, in articles or letters in the "Quarterly Review", or in books, some published by the Fellowship (see Chapter 10), some independently, all adding to the considerable weight of examples available for study. Much of this had to do with communication with the departed, the controversial aspect of the subject already dealt with in previous chapters.[10] Putting on one side the theological issues, a great deal of this material was of a high quality, and already subjected to much analysis on the part of the recipients, or those involved in publishing. Florence West Pell's book "Death Has No Sting" is a classic example of this type of production,[11] but undoubtedly "Testimony of Light", communications from Frances Banks to Helen Greaves, is the outstanding example which has stood the test of time and proved by its continuing demand that it has something serious to give to many Christian readers.[12]

This type of work cannot in itself lead (to quote the Rt. Rev. Mervyn Stockwood, formerly Bishop of Southwark, and for many years a CFPSS Patron): "to a belief in God. The acceptance of the reality of God depends on other factors. What psychical investigation can do is to drive a coach and four through a crudely materialistic view which assumes that life on this planet is the sum total of human experience, instead of seeing it as part of something greater in the context of an evolutionary process and of an extension of personal and collective consciousness."[13]

From many references in his writings (and this was confirmed by Bishop Stockwood in an interview kindly given in May 1991) it is apparent that he attaches real value in certain circumstances to the phenomenon of communication with the discarnate through a "developed psychic" (his own phrase), always stressing the necessity for absolute integrity in the sensitive, and of the true need of the person seeking help; (in the case of a Christian this need having to be demonstrably beyond the help of faith held at the time). In these circumstances Bishop Stockwood confirmed that he has found that comfort and strength can be received through such a meeting of two states of consciousness.

In 1979 the "Christian Parapsychologist"[14] published the full text of the Lang Report (the enquiry into Spiritualism chaired by Dr Francis Underhill, with all the inherent implications of communication with the departed, already mentioned in Chapters 2 and 3). Valuable comment followed in several later issues; and a detailed survey by the Rev. Angus Haddow of psychical research and the churches.[15] In 1982, to regularise as much as possible what might be deemed to be the CFPSS view on this complex question, the Council produced a statement on mediumship, with an introduction by Chancellor E. Garth Moore.[16] It has been found helpful to republish most of the foregoing in leaflet form.

These subjects remain of perennial interest, always with new aspects coming to the fore. Thus the work of Dr Moody and his successors in connection with the "near-death experience" has made a valid contribution to the question of the viability of human personality after death in a spiritual context.[17] The Rev. Charles Fryer has continued to make a contribution through his own experiences and studies on the subject of post mortem communication.[18] Mrs Enid Case has collected and presented some remarkable examples of supernatural scentings.[19] In 1979 the Rev. Alun Virgin chaired working parties on the question of mediumship and the pastoral implications of psi. Sadly his premature death prevented that work coming to fruition, although a preliminary report was prepared and circulated to Council. Two books by the Rev. Allan Barham, fortunately written before his withdrawal from the active scene, are useful sources for those wanting an overall view of the range of psychic phenomena.[20]

Perhaps it would be true to say that the main onus of keeping the CFPSS supplied with information and material has now passed to the "Christian Parapsychologist", of which a fuller account will be given in Chapter 8. It could also be said that the work has become more reflective than active. Again to quote Rhea White: "Maybe the gift of an exceptional human experience is a call to transcendence";[21] and Christian parapsychology inevitably reflects the response to this call. Meanwhile the "Christian Parapsychologist" continues to act as a bridge between science and religion, the most dearly held aim of Reginald Lester and many other founding members. Yet much of value has gone before and must be part of the whole. For more detailed access to all the work carried out since those early days, the archives of the "Quarterly Review" will remain a rich source for future students.

CHAPTER 6

The CFPSS and Prayer and Mysticism

From the earliest days of the Fellowship until the present a spiritual approach to psychical and religious studies has been deemed to be a pre-requisite; and the practice of prayer and meditation, and seeking to understand the mystical element in religious experience have always been important strands in CFPSS commitment.

Many members, both clergy and lay, throughout its existence have contributed to this part of the work, in lectures, writings and group leadership, but two names, Frances Banks and Martin Israel, stand out in this aspect of CFPSS development. While never minimising the importance of sacramental and congregational worship as a vital part of Christian life, each demonstrated and taught from the beginning of membership of the CFPSS a personal dedication to the prayer of quiet and the inner experience, in the relationship between the individual and God, that relationship ever to be based on Jesus Christ and the Holy Spirit.

This was the foundation upon which both Frances Banks and Martin Israel based their psychic knowledge and advice and counsel for others. The paths by which they came to this point of their lives were different but converged at the appropriate time in a remarkable and fruitful way, so that as Frances Banks came to the relinquishing of her earthly existence Martin Israel was ready to take up the work and carry it through.

Frances Banks was born in 1892 into a family of divergent beliefs ranging from the agnosticism of her father to the ardent Christian evangelism of missionary relatives. Dreams of a terrifying downpouring of power, and an uplifting experience of the Holy Spirit during her confirmation were early demonstrations that Frances was to follow the path of the natural mystic. A degree and a teaching diploma provided the opportunity for an independent life at a time when this would not have been the normal path for one from her family background. Some teaching experience followed, but gradually a deeper religious vocation was manifesting, and eventually a year of instruction at a missionary college was followed by her entry, in 1921, into an Anglican religious order, that of the Community of the Resurrection in Grahamstown, South Africa. The setting of this life was a rigorous spiritual and practical routine, based on the three vows of poverty, chastity and obedience. Later she was to become Assistant Lecturer at Grahamstown Training College, and later still the Principal of that College. Those years, from 1921 until 1946, she was to describe as an absorbing and wholly satisfying test of experience and the reality of the call to service.

However, she felt that there was more to be done than she had yet achieved, and it was as if an inner voice insisted, "unphenomenally but incontestably: why had I not even begun to do the work for which I had been called?"[1] It was a visiting lecturer to the College who shattered her ignorance. "There followed fascinating accounts of notable teachers in Johannesburg who were demonstrating new powers of the mind for healing and happiness. These accounts were supplemented by demonstrations of posture, and of relaxation therapies, yielding some remarkable results in healing. Concurrently I became aware of an unusual state of consciousness in times of meditation and Holy Communion. It was as though my spirit shook free of the body and rose spirally as if on wings. The experience was formless and unemotional, inspiring and immeasurably refreshing. It had a crystalline spiritual quality, unlike the heavily-laden downpour of the early days. It was not that power poured down but rather that some detachable part of me floated up."[2]

Impelled to follow these leadings, Frances spoke fully and frankly to her very supportive Mother Superior. Time was given to get away for quietness in the beautiful countryside, and the first experience of (her own term) "etheric vision" occurred. "It seemed that perhaps by a heightened reaction to swifter vibrations, the sense-organs themselves could apprehend the living matrix of a subtler physical life, functioning at all times, whether visible or not, ever in flux, permeating and uniting all the life of the planet in a single network; basis of brotherhood, of healing, and perhaps of many another miracle."[3]

As her studies widened to embrace esoteric as well as traditional spirituality, so the visionary side of her life developed, leading to the request for leave from the Order for further research and study purposes. Eventually, and perhaps inevitably, after a period of sadness and heart-searching on her part and of those concerned with her religious life, Frances was released from her vows and returned to England.

Here she found her natural working fulfilment as Tutor Organiser in Maidstone Prison in time to take part in the "Maidstone Experiment" in prison education, from which came her book "Teach Them to Live".[4] Of this Lord Birkett wrote: "This excellent book contributes to the treatment of prisoners in knowledge, vision and faith"; and it has been said that the book should be the bible of prison reform.

Parallel to this work Frances continued to hold her dream of a university for spiritual studies, but at last realised that a more limited objective might be the "one step enough", and so, seeing the newspaper notice of the formation of a Churches' Fellowship for Psychical Study she recognised the opening offered and became a founder member, and was soon on Council and the Research Committee. Inevitably she was swept up into a cycle of activity, addressing and meeting people at every stage of enquiry from within the fold of institutional Christianity and from the fields of education and science where so many had drifted away from the practice of religion.

None who heard her speak in those days could forget the visual and spiritual impact of her 'presence'. After relinquishing the habit of her Order she had at first reluctantly and then enjoyably learned to manage her hair and clothes with style; and amethyst, her favourite shade, enhanced the blue of her deep-set eyes. Above all, there was the effect of the passionate sincerity of her beliefs and of the brilliant spirit which shone through her.

So all her study, dedication, discipline and spiritual development to date found its purpose, and for the rest of her life, until 1965, this was to be the outlet for her inspiration and vocation, in teaching meditation, conducting retreats, giving spiritual guidance, and conveying to all who listened her conviction that in mysticism lay the ultimate healing.

In April, 1965, the culmination of this work was the setting up of a new Mysticism Committee. Preparatory private group work had already taken place for some years previously, as reported in ~~1953~~.[5] The new committee, under the terms of reference proposed by Frances Banks, had more precise aims: (1) to produce books or pamphlets on the subject of meditation: (2) to define where the psychic ends and the spiritual begins: and (3) to interpret the bearing of mysticism on the present world.

That first meeting was held in April, 1965, and others followed, but sadly in November of the same year, Frances died. However, another remarkably gifted person was ready to carry on the work, being present at that first meeting, taking the meditation which closed it, and progressing eventually to lead the Committee until it closed, and to do far more than that.

At that time, Dr Martin Israel (as he then was) was not so well known in the Fellowship, although he had already embarked on the course which was to make him a widely respected spiritual authority. He was born in Johannesburg, in 1927. There he studied medicine before coming to England in 1951, and it is interesting to realise that while he was following his medical studies in Johannesburg, Frances Banks, too, was there, rounding off her religious life and entering the wider world of spiritual studies. However at that time their paths did not cross.

Martin Israel, as his name must indicate, was born a Jew, and was brought up in the Jewish faith, but in the liberal tradition. There were early indications of the spiritual path he was to tread. In his own words: "Synagogue worship was a joy to me, and I was well aware of the presence of God when the sacred Scroll of the Law was presented, unrolled, and read during the most holy part of the service. I am very grateful that I was brought up in the Jewish religion, which I still regard as the central manifestation and guardian of God's self-revelation to man. Never at any time did I submit to the temptation of changing my name with its religious overtones, for I knew that both its glory and its burden were part of my heritage, and one that had to be both acknowledged and redeemed. In fact I suffered minimally from anti-Semitic prejudice, unlike my unfortunate relatives in Lithuania, all of whom were burnt alive in their village synagogue by the Nazis during the early part of the Russian campaign.

"And yet Christ disclosed Himself to me when I was scarcely out of infancy. I could never escape from Him even had I been so inclined. I began to see Him both as the consummation of all that Judaism had taught and witnessed, and also the power of God universalised to all men, of all races. I knew that though He was a man as I was, in Him the power of God shone eternally, and He was in His life and witness to the truth the manifestation of the one God in the flesh."[6]

So, gradually, he moved from Judaism to Christianity, while in post-graduate studies, National Service, lecturing in his specialty (pathology) at the Royal College of Surgeons, and hospital consultancy, he painfully acquired the speaking skills which would be used so brilliantly and inspirationally in his capacity of spiritual teacher. In "Precarious Living", quoted above, he writes with agonising honesty of his difficulties in his early days. However, all the while the spring of mysticism was flowing through him, as it had from early childhood. Eventually as he became first Vice Chairman, then Chairman of the Fellowship, his religious life was deepening, to embrace ordination in the Anglican Church, in 1975; and so he widened still further his tremendous ministry of healing, counselling, deliverance and spiritual and retreat direction.

Like Frances Banks, Martin Israel was no stranger to the more esoteric aspects of world religions and spiritual cults. However, at first under the Presidency of Chancellor Garth Moore and then during his own tenure as President he took a far stronger line than Frances might have done (although that can only be speculation) concerning the dangers of giving importance to that side of spiritual experience. This was not always acceptable to all the membership of the CFPSS, and during the chairmanship of the late Rev. Dr Kenneth Cuming, (a gifted psychic and devoted follower of the Christian healing ministry, and for several years first Chaplain and then Warden of the Dorothy Kerin Home of Healing at Burrswood), a much wider interpretation of spiritual matters, while still maintaining allegiance to the traditional churches, was promoted. However, support for Martin Israel's more uncompromising views was in the majority, and in all his speaking and writing he continued to point ever more firmly to the supreme channel of grace, the Holy Spirit.

Meanwhile, from 1965, following the death of Frances Banks, the Mysticism Committee continued its work, at first under the chairmanship of the Rev. Richard Hall, and then from September, 1971 under Martin Israel. The late Vera Staff, who was a member of the Mysticism Committee from its second meeting, and for many years the Secretary, said of those early days: "It was considered by Frances to be important that members should be able to exchange ideas with other people; that they should accept mysticism as the ultimate form of healing; appreciate the use of silence in community and with others; encourage people to study mysticism for themselves, and bear in mind the ideal of service."[7]

Above all, Frances Banks was a teacher, and one of her most cherished aims, the publication of informative and inspiring books and booklets, was fully realised by the Mysticism Committee. In a talk given to the London group of the Fellowship, the late Jean Sydney (a long-time friend of Frances and hard-working and loyal supporter of the CFPSS until the end of her life) said: "She was writing a book which was never completed, on Saints and other remarkable people, before she died. She left her papers to me, amongst which I found four completed chapters of this book, on Teresa of Avila, St. John of the Cross, Plotinus and Teilhard de Chardin. The Mysticism Committee published these chapters as our first booklet."[8]

Many others followed, some written by individual members of the Committee, others jointly by the Committee. Two by Martin Israel were: "An Approach to Spirituality", and "An Approach to Mysticism", the latter being the text of six lectures given at the College of Psychic Studies. C.E. Bignall wrote: "The Intuitive Faculty", and Vera Staff: "On Forming a Group for the Study of Meditation". The Committee produced "About Death", "About Prayer", and "Guidelines for Meditation". Vera Staff wrote a series of articles for the "Quarterly Review" on the mystical poets, and some of these were produced in booklet form. She also wrote a valuable book on dreams.[9] Independently of the Fellowship but woven into his work as an inspired speaker, Martin Israel was to go on to write a sequence of books on spiritual and mystical themes which were to be widely read and continually in demand.

Articles in the "Quarterly Review" kept up the theme, emphasising the importance of prayer and the practice of meditation, with contributions on the mysticism of the saints, as with St Francis of Assisi and St Thérèse of Lisieux, and other allied subjects such as speaking with tongues, the children of Fatima, and the experience of pilgrimage. In September, 1988 a whole issue was devoted to the theme of mystical (peak) experiences.

So, through conference addresses, services and meditations, and Branch or Regional retreats, and through the journals of the CFPSS and other literature, the study and practice of prayer and meditation in the context of Christian healing and spirituality have become established as the strongest strands in the Fellowship tradition. The majority of members find this to be a vital side of their religious life and are encouraged and inspired to follow this Christian path as the sure way to be in touch with the inner levels of being. The work has been and continues to be passed on to other groups within the CFPSS or within local churches or other organisations, so that it is hoped that in this way the Fellowship gives back to the Christian body much of the blessing it has received through the dedication and devotion of pioneering members.

CHAPTER 7

The CFPSS and the Churches

The relationship between the Fellowship and the Church as a whole has been, inevitably, touched on in most if not all the preceding chapters. However, that relationship is so fundamental to the Fellowship that it is worth looking at the question in a chronological way, as well as within the various branches of the subject already considered.

What has been apparent, right from the start, is the determination of the founding members, predominantly clergy, that the CFPSS should be constituted, organised and maintained in accordance with the carefully chosen wording of its title and its original aims and objects. These set out a Fellowship, within the churches, of Christians who wished to know more of psychical phenomena past and present, their value, meaning and purpose, linking this study with the gifts of the Holy Spirit to the church, "the blessed company of all faithful people". In establishing this aim the Council insisted on involving people of some standing and authority in the church. In those very early days there were frequent contributions from such as Dean Matthews of St. Paul's, and the early and continuing recruitment of senior clergy as vice presidents (later to be called patrons).

If the senior clergy in those early days, and still today, mainly represent the Anglican church, there was and is no intention of exclusiveness in Fellowship policy, with other denominations always well represented, if regrettably less numerously. The pattern of membership set up required that applicants for full membership should be practising members of churches belonging or affiliated to the World Council of Churches or must themselves acknowledge Jesus Christ as Lord and Saviour of the world. This meant that only committed Christians could be full members and thus hold office. This was a wise and necessary means of ensuring that the newly established Fellowship could not be taken over and controlled by the many enthusiastic spiritualist or psychic researchers who did not give priority to a Christian commitment as required in the traditional churches, and who did not always appreciate the value of that priority. The Minutes of a 1956 Council meeting give a good example of this. The Rev. Maurice Elliott, speaking about the appointment of a new member of Council, reported that he (Mr. Elliott) had been assured that "he believed in what we believe, but, no sooner had he become a member of Council, than he wrote to me as follows: 'I admit that I have done a certain amount of fencing and temporising with you over the Christological question. You asked me at our last lunch whether I thought Christ was/is unique, and I answered in the affirmative. But, you see, I think we are all unique'." The gentleman in question received a very sharp dismissal.[1]

Always there was this balance to be sought, of keeping within the framework of accepted contemporary theology, with many articles in the "Quarterly Review" on the subject, while trying to widen the recognition of work done by scientists, psychologists and parapsychologists. Always the general theme was of the importance of theological study and ecclesiastical participation.

Of course one of the obvious problems was that theology varies from church to church, according to denomination and churchmanship, as exemplified in the early days of the Fellowship (and still nowadays) with permissible varying interpretations of the doctrine of prayers for the dead. That major differences can be entertained within one "church" is demonstrated at this moment by the controversies over the ordination of women. Fortunately that is not something which comes within the sphere of the CFPSS.

In 1977 Canon Pearce-Higgins was making reference to "the field of theological controversy with whose tortuous complexities most of the laity were unfamiliar", and again, describing the early days, to "tough committee meetings in which the clerical members united as a body on theological grounds"; and to "dear Dean Matthews who sometimes found our lack of theological expertise somewhat alarming"; or again: "I can remember being shouted down by a large gathering of clergy at Southampton when I dared mention the etheric body"! He continued (speaking of Col. Lester), "It would seem that the Powers that be chose wisely when they laid this burden not on a professional theologian or priest but on a professional journalist and propagandist who was far better placed as a sincere layman to launch an assault on cherished ideas, than on those who could be subject to the bogeys of Episcopal sanction and ecclesiastical protocol. I like to think of Reg in his prime as a fine English gentleman, with his excellent war record, his esteemed position as a doyen of journalists, his many-sided personal gifts, his charm and courtesy; perhaps no more suitable 'apostle' could have been found to set this particular ball rolling."[2]

While speaking of the somewhat easier position of the lay Christian in this context, Canon Pearce-Higgins does not belabour the invidious position of the clergy, but we who have followed on in the Fellowship can and do acknowledge their pioneer spirit and courage. Remaining within the churches, while pursuing the study rôle of the Fellowship, was certainly no easy option, but that is what the CFPSS was committed to from the start, and nothing has changed since.

As always there have been the branch meetings and conferences and articles in the quarterly journals, with either agreement or argument, and hopefully developments following in the minds of speakers and writers as well as in the listeners or readers. There have been clergy conferences, such as in 1956 at the College of St Mark and St John in Chelsea, and again in October 1970 in the Chapter House at Southwark.

In 1962 the Annual Conference, held at Lincoln College, Oxford, was described in the "Baptist Times" as a "feast of reason and a flow of soul". At the same time the West Country conference in Torquay was reported as having 100 attending the opening service with an address from the Bishop of Crediton, the Rt Rev Wilfrid Westall, in which he spoke of the ministry of the 'unseen ones' and of angels and 'messengers' acting as intermediaries in bringing the realisation of the wonderful work of God to this earth in the age of space and insecurity.

In March 1963 the change of title took place (to include

the word 'spiritual'), and this was reported (as based on a referendum of members) together with the encouraging message from the Archbishop of Canterbury, as quoted in Chapter 2. In September 1965 a Theology Committee was inaugurated under the leadership of the Rev. Donald Bretherton who has produced so much fine work since that time. Throughout all these early years the Fellowship was playing an important part in encouraging and supporting the growth of the Ministry of Healing within the churches; and in meeting others who recognised the gifts of the Holy Spirit. For example, in the "Quarterly Review" of September, 1964, a reference was made to a forthcoming talk from the Rev. Michael Harper "former Curate of All Souls, Langham Place, who is now doing free-lance work as a writer and lecturer on charismatic renewal and other gifts of the Spirit within the Church". This was another area in which the CFPSS had its own special contribution to make, although not always in full accordance with the theology of the charismatic movement.

In 1970 the CFPSS Book Club (see Chapter 10) published an important book by the Rev. Leonard Argyle entitled "Nothing to Hide: The Great Prohibition (Deut. Chapter 18)". In this book the writer, acknowledging the help of the Rev. Donald Bretherton, set out to deal with the Biblical interpretations and translations which have caused so much limitation and confusion in Christian understanding.[3]

In September 1970 the "Quarterly Review" carried an article on "The CFPSS and The Churches" in which the present writer set out the arguments for the importance of Fellowship members remaining faithful in their prior commitment to the traditional churches.[4] In a subsequent issue, Col. Lester commented that no other article in his experience of "the Review" had brought such a flood of supportive letters, indicating that the bulk of Fellowship members remained true to the original purpose.

In December, 1972 the Rev. Alun and Mrs. Margaret Virgin wrote a joint contribution reflecting the pressures building up as the more esoteric and occult organisations began to increase in numbers and inevitably attempt (mostly with the best of motives) to hold cross-membership with the CFPSS. The Virgins' article set out all the arguments most cogently, ending with the words: "The Fellowship with its specialised knowledge and interest can deepen and enrich the spiritual life of the Churches. The Churches have much indeed to offer members of the Fellowship in a wider framework of worship and teaching. It would be disastrous for the Fellowship to become just another 'fringe group'. By its very nature and constitution it cannot be spiritually self-sufficient. It is an auxiliary to, not a substitute for, the Churches whose support it seeks."[5] Again, in September 1973, the Rev. Dr Kenneth Cuming, then chairman, wrote strongly along similar lines. Although Dr Cuming's interpretation of Christianity and New Age issues was very different from that of the Rev. Alun Virgin and others, and he was himself a centre of some controversy, he remained convinced that the only place for CFPSS members was within the church which is the Body of Christ.

Then in July 1975 Dr Martin Israel became Chairman having recently been ordained into the Anglican church. Now the Rev. Dr Martin Israel, he was already well known in the Fellowship through his work with the Mysticism Committee and his inspirational speaking gifts, and from March 1972 as Vice Chairman. As Chairman he was to make, with the President, Chancellor Garth Moore, and ably supported by the then General Secretary, Maurice Frost, a formidable leadership team in all matters theological and ecclesiastical. This was, many must feel, truly providential, for the 70s and 80s were to be the years of the 'occult explosion', the enormous growth of many esoteric and fringe spiritual activities. Strong and informed leadership was exactly what was necessary for a society such as the CFPSS. Not only was it attacked from without but also from within as individuals, branches and, in one case an enthusiastic but misguided official of the CFPSS (Scotland) (for an account of this separate body see Chapter 9) felt drawn to oppose what they saw as ecclesiasticism, 'churchianity', and entrenched orthodoxy at the centre of the Fellowship. Most of these attacks were the result of sincerely held beliefs, although as always it is necessary to look behind the sincerest of motives to see what darker forces are at work in all human manifestations.

One of the darkest pages in church history must be the persecution of so-called witches. For several centuries thousands of innocent, if often foolish or ignorant people were tortured and killed by burning and other means, for fear of witchcraft. That witchcraft existed, and still does today, no one could deny, but until the repeal of the Witchcraft Act in 1736 unbelievable horrors were perpetrated in the name of the church and the law. People with natural psychic, intuitive, or healing gifts suffered with other innocents as well as some who might well have been guilty.[6] Little wonder that there runs a deep seam of fear and resentment against religious authority in those who carry within them similar gifts and the seeds of remembrance. Yet no one can welcome the increase of cults and sects which prey upon the credulous and the vulnerable; and many who, within the Fellowship, work in the ministry of deliverance fully recognise that spiritual darkness is by no means eradicated.

In this the Fellowship has allied itself with the church and continues to do so, while maintaining the integrity of its recognition of the gift of 'discernment of spirits', the gift most often misunderstood and decried. That gift includes the discernment of good spirits, as well as bad, and in the ministry to the bereaved such a gift used with discrimination can be a source of comfort;[7] and it can be part of the ministry of healing to the spiritual environment as mentioned by Bishop Maddocks and quoted in Chapter 3.

The tensions of the 1970s, with the ferment within the church with the growth of the evangelical wing, and outside, with the growth of New Age philosophies, led to parallel tensions within the CFPSS. As a result of the tightening up of the adherence to traditional doctrine, many members broke away to set up or join other organisations, leaving a smaller but less divided membership to carry on into the 80s and 90s. Meanwhile positive work continued, such as the appearance of such books as Michael Perry's "The Resurrection of Man"[8] and Morton Kelsey's "The Christian and the Supernatural".[9] In September, 1979 Michael Perry lectured in Bradford Cathedral on psychic research, and in December, 1980 the Rev. Angus Haddow, of the CFPSS (Scotland), produced a comprehensive paper for the "Christian Parapsychologist" on "The Churches and Psychical Research" (see Chapter 5). A Christian theology which embraces the human experiences so widely recognised in the work of the CFPSS and the Religious Experience Research Unit (now the Alister Hardy Research Centre) is surely the long-awaited development of the current time.

Annual conferences are held, when possible in cathedral cities, or in teacher or theological training colleges, with invited participation from local clergy and staff. In recent years clergy conferences, or visits by Fellowship officers to local chapter or other clergy meetings, have been frequent occurrences. The main limitation of growth stems not from lack of interest or response but from current sociological factors governing the working lives and leisure of most people, clergy and lay alike; but the work, in faithfulness, goes on.

Two quotations seem apt to end this chapter. The first from the Ven. Michael Perry, Editor of the "Christian Parapsychologist" and currently Chairman, who in his letter to the Fellowship in 1987 said: "We in the Churches' Fellowship may not be up to the theological acrobatics of the professionals, but we must hold to the sanctity of our experience. When we are quizzed as to the value of psychical gifts of which we have evidence, we should not be sidetracked but should come out with: 'one thing I know – whereas I was blind now I see'."[10]

And let the last words go to one of our brave pioneers, Canon John Pearce-Higgins. "Those who believe in the Love of God, in that quality in which it was revealed to us in the life, teaching, death and Resurrection of Jesus Christ, have no need to fear new discoveries or new truths, but will know that each new widening of our horizons only discloses new details, new wonders, new heights and depths in the providential workings of that God and Father who was in Christ Jesus reconciling the world to himself, and from whose love in Christ nothing in heaven or earth can ever separate us. Until the churches give some clear teaching on these great and supremely vital subjects of life and death we shall not command the respect or win the support of the people who expect us to be able to enlighten them on these problems. 'For if the trumpet give an uncertain sound, who shall prepare himself in the battle?'"[11]

CHAPTER 8

The CFPSS and Christian Parapsychology

In Chapter 5 it was shown that a great deal of work had been done by the CFPSS in connection with psychical research. Why then is it necessary to devote a chapter to parapsychology, and, further, why 'Christian' parapsychology? In the closing lines of Chapter 5 the suggestion was made that the rôle of Christian parapsychology is to reflect the call to transcendence arising out of the gift of exceptional human experiences; and in the past few decades the word parapsychology has in fact gradually overtaken the use of the term 'psychical research'. According to the Oxford English Dictionary 'parapsychology' is "the science or study of phenomena which lie outside the sphere of orthodox psychology", and the earliest usage of the term seems to have been in the 1920s. In the 1950s, when the Fellowship was founded, the term 'psychical research' was still the more familiar, though the trend was developing towards placing more emphasis on human personality and psychology while still studying paranormal phenomena or 'psi'; and as early as 1956 the Parapsychological Foundation of New York made a grant to the CFPSS in recognition of its work and aims.

By 1964 Canon John Pearce-Higgins, in an enthusiastic review of a book by Edward C. Barker, spoke of the author's interpretation of the Christian faith "in the light of his own psychological and parapsychological knowledge";[1] in 1966, he (John Pearce-Higgins) attended an international conference on parapsychology in Konstanz, Germany, presenting his paper in German;[2] and in June 1970 a note in the "Quarterly Review" stated that the Parapsychological Foundation in New York had been accepted for affiliation to the American Association for the Advancement of Science.

Other references denote the acceptance of such studies in British universities (such as Oxford and Edinburgh), and from

Edinburgh Professor John Beloff wrote: "The computer analogy which now dominates cognitive psychology has created a conception of man as an information-processing system which has become the mainstay of the modern materialistic view of mind. On the other side, parapsychology alone can provide empirical support for the transcendent view of mind. So long, however, as the parapsychological evidence is open to question, the contest is bound to be an uneven one. It is an astounding fact that, a century after the founding of the Society for Psychical Research, there is still a total lack of consensus regarding the actuality of any parapsychological phenomena."[3] Obviously more than a purely scientific approach was required, and this the Church of Scotland (among other bodies) tried to remedy with its General Assembly Working Party on Parapsychology, in 1975, under the chairmanship of the Rev. Max Magee, a member of CFPSS (Scotland).

The CFPSS certainly affirmed its acceptance of the concept of a Christian approach to parapsychology with the establishment of its second journal, the "Christian Parapsychologist". The event is dealt with below, but meanwhile, to jump ahead a little, a quotation from the (by then) editor, Michael Perry, perhaps gives a good explanation of the necessary participation of the Christian in the field of parapsychology. Having listed the many enquiries by different church bodies into relevant matters, such as spiritualism, prayer for the departed, exorcism and occult and psychic activities, including the 1939 Lang Report, the Editorial continued: "The field is wider than it was in 1939, and parapsychology as a scientific discipline has not stood still in the last forty years. Christians still seek guidance, and the Churches' Fellowship and the 'Christian Parapsychologist' attempt to help them to be aware of studies in this field and to think through the doctrinal and personal issues which they raise."[4]

In this context it will be realised that the founding of the "Christian Parapsychologist" was a major development in CFPSS work, and it arose, as have other such developments, in the coming together of the right people at the right time, under what must be seen by those with faith as divine inspiration.

So now it is necessary to look at two at least of the major

personalities involved. The first of these is the late Margaret Brice-Smith, who died in 1989 at the age of 96, never having lost her love of and enthusiasm for the work of the Fellowship. She was a founder member and thereafter was continuously involved in the work of building up several groups or branches, the library, and the Mysticism Committee. She remained a Vice President until her death. The daughter of an Anglican clergyman, and highly intelligent, she nevertheless had to follow the path of most women of her class and time in staying at home and not pursuing any form of higher education. The loss of a beloved brother in World War I, followed by a psychic experience of friends, concerning his death, made very clear to her the poverty of the traditional church view of such experiences. In fact, she was told by her clergyman father that it was dangerous and of the devil, and she obediently but sadly put such ideas on one side. What was her joy to hear, a full generation later, of the establishment of a fellowship designed specifically to foster, within the Christian church, a more enlightened but still critical response to such experiences. She joined the Churches' Fellowship for Psychical Study (as it was then) and gave it her enthusiastic support until the end of her life.

In the words of Martin Israel: "Perhaps the greatest contribution of Margaret to the Fellowship was her ardent support for Leslie Price in his striving for a truly parapsychological Christian journal. The "Quarterly Review" was, and remains, an indispensable house journal, but by its very nature it could not easily venture into deeper technical paths. And so, by the vision of these two pioneers, the "Christian Parapsychologist" was launched, a journal which, in my opinion, is one of the most important ecumenical publications of the present time."[5]

Leslie Price had graduated from Sussex University in 1968 with an honours degree in religious studies. Following an already well established interest in the paranormal (inspired in him as a sixth former by the books of Raynor Johnson), he became involved in many appropriate societies. He met Margaret Brice-Smith through the Youth Group of the CFPSS, which she ran with Mrs Gwen Bacon, and at the College of Psychic Studies. His interest was to develop into a considerable knowledge both of the field of parapsychology and the workers in it, and by 1975 he was member of the CFPSS Committee for the Study of Psychical Phenomena.

In a guest editorial in the "Christian Parapsychologist" in September, 1985, (ten years after its first issue), he described the origins of the journal. An idea had kept him wakeful into the night before a meeting of the Psychical Phenomena Committee, and at that meeting he was able to suggest putting out a newsletter on an experimental basis, and this was agreed. The proposed publication was to carry not only "doings of members of the committee in the research field but also review Christian attempts to come to terms with the paranormal in the world at large." The article makes it clear that several people were involved in the early success of the idea, including the Rev. Allan Barham, Chairman of the Committee, Michael Lewis, Edwin Butler, and David Ellis, who acted as Assistant Editor and was responsible for the design and printing at his own printing press where the title "The Christian Parapsychologist" emerged in discussion, and the logo (the Chi-Ro with Psi superimposed) was devised; all this in time for the first edition, under the editorship of Leslie Price, in September, 1975.

Support was needed in other ways and Margaret Brice-Smith was soon much involved, with financial assistance, and as circulation manager (assisted by Mrs Jean Sydney). This was necessary at first as the new journal was seen by some as a threat to the existing "Quarterly Review", and for a few issues the "Christian Parapsychologist" was produced semi-independently with the title registered as a business name. However, it soon became clear that the new publication had great potential value for the work of the CFPSS, and by September 1977 it had been agreed that the new journal was to become an official publication of the Fellowship, distributed with the "Quarterly Review". Leslie Price was to continue as Editor, at the same time becoming joint editor of the "Quarterly Review" with Maurice Frost, both of which editorships he continued to hold until September, 1978.

During this period another important name was to be added to the roll call of Fellowship workers, although this was not the first time that that name had appeared in CFPSS publications. In the "Quarterly Review" in 1959, John Pearce-Higgins contributed a review of "The Easter Enigma" by the (then) Rev.

Michael Perry. Although not all the arguments in the book were acceptable to the reviewer, as a whole the notice was very favourable, saying: "This is the first large-scale attempt by a clergyman of the Church of England to apply some of the findings of psychic science or parapsychology to the narratives of the bible. 'The Easter Enigma' is valuable because Mr Perry is fresh from taking a first-class degree in Natural Science and Theology at Cambridge, an unusual combination, and therefore he may be presumed to know what he is talking about in both fields."[6] ("The Easter Enigma" and its author were also very favourably mentioned in a book by Renée Haynes of the same period).[7]

Eighteen years later, in 1977, in the eighth number of the "Christian Parapsychologist", Leslie Price as Editor reported that Michael Perry (by then the Venerable Michael Perry and Archdeacon of Durham, with previous valuable publishing experience), had accepted an invitation to become book reviews editor and a member of the editorial group. In 1978, when Leslie Price felt he had to give up as Editor, Michael Perry was ready to take over, and he has continued as Editor to date, now combining that function with that of Chairmanship of the Fellowship, while still holding the position of Archdeacon of Durham and numerous other appointments of importance in the church. Since then the "Christian Parapsychologist" has continued to grow in weight, both figuratively and in fact, and to make an important contribution to the work of the Fellowship in the field of parapsychology, with particular emphasis on its relevance to spiritual or religious questions.

To do justice to the range and variety of subjects covered in the sixteen years that the journal has existed would entail the production of a list of titles too long for this short history, but the following may convey some idea, bearing in mind that all subjects are considered from the Christian viewpoint: healing in various forms; medicine and religion; pastoral care in psychic troubles; trance in Holy Scripture; mediaeval mystical phenomena; deliverance and exorcism; the transcendent in parapsychology; prophecy; angels; OBEs and NDEs; reincarnation; Swedenborg; Padre Pio; Sai Baba; witches and shamans; saints and the psychical and mystical; science and religion. One of the subjects covered in depth has been that of parapsychology in education, with the production by a CFPSS working party, chaired by Miss Barbara Gadd, of a booklet entitled "Parapsychology in Education". In all of the subjects the approach of the writers has been serious and critical; there have been numerous book reviews, many by eminent clergy and scholars, and mention of many books received (not necessarily recommended). Lively correspondence and a regular detailed index add to the worth of the production.

Perhaps the best way to sum up the work of the "Christian Parapsychologist" is to quote some thoughts of the Editor as expressed in a report to the Annual General Meeting of the Fellowship at Digby Stuart College, Roehampton in 1982. He said: "We try to combine theological sophistication with readability, and are nothing like so abstruse as many of the articles in the "Clergy Review" or "Expository Times" or "Theology", to mention only three of the most widely-read professional journals of the priest or minister. A clergyman should therefore find CP well within his professional competence to assimilate, but we also try to ensure that there is nothing in it which is below his dignity to be taken as a serious contribution to theological understanding of this marvellous and mysterious world within which we are set."[8]

The contributions to the "Christian Parapsychologist" have often included valuable material from our American counterparts, many of these being papers delivered at the three conferences on Christian Parapsychology, (two International and one Ecumenical) held by the Fellowship in 1978, 1984 and 1990 respectively, once again the idea originating from Leslie Price. These conferences have followed on from the CFPSS annual conferences in each of the years noted, and have been interesting and valuable opportunities for encounters with those involved in Christian parapsychology in this and other countries, as well as a source of contributions to the journal. Other exchanges have taken place through visits abroad, such as that of Canon Pearce-Higgins to Germany (already mentioned), and by Michael Perry, Leslie Price and others to America and Rome. Many CFPSS members belong to or hold office in comparable organisations. For example, one of our Vice Presidents, Miss Renée Haynes, has also been a distinguished officer of the Society for Psychical Research for many years; and Hugh Corbett, CFPSS Vice Chairman, belongs to the Society for Psychical Research and several British and international societies with scientific, religious, healing and psychical research interests, following very closely meetings and journals, making his own contribution from time to time.

Let some thoughts from a contribution by a CFPSS member at the 1990 Ecumenical Conference on Christian Parapsychology bring together some useful concepts for the purpose of this chapter. Professor Max Payne, Lecturer (now retired) in Education and Religious Studies at Sheffield City Polytechnic, was speaking to the conference under the title: "The Necessity of Parapsychology". Having looked at correspondences between cosmology, quantum physics and mathematics, and the consciousness of the nature mystic or the visionary, he said: "The whole lesson of science is that there is no final structure, and everything evolves and changes. And so the investigation of the materialist hypothesis of consciousness may well leave materialism to self-destruct, but it points religion in the direction of open religion. I prove none of these points, I merely suggest them – it faces the Christian, specifically the Christian, I think, with the problem of whether Christianity is a living religion or a dead religion. Those of us who think it is a living religion are therefore prepared to enter a process of profound re-interpretation." In question time he also said: "If everything is possible, structure and order are necessary in order to have coherence and meaning, so not only do we have to always return to this ordered structured world but we should not dispose of too many of our structures, which include the church, in the process of dealing with the terrifying openness of reality."[9]

Parapsychology it seems then may indeed be offering that structure, that bridge between science and religion, the concept which will have been met more than once already in this development of the history of the CFPSS.

CHAPTER 9

Fellow Members and Pilgrims

The preceding chapter was mostly concerned with intellectual concepts and, as with all other chapters so far, inevitably it dealt with the best-known leaders and speakers. This chapter is the one in which to look at those who followed on, who implemented the original inspiration, fleshed out the abstract ideas, gave day to day humanity to the theories and theologies, and who built the bridges, so often talked about, and themselves crossed and re-crossed them as they were built. Reginald Lester saw those bridges as between "the theologian and the scientist, between the spiritual healer and the physician; and between those inside the church and those outside;"[1] and perhaps it would be right to include that other very important area of bridging, between this world and the next, or between the physical dimension and the spiritual.

As has already been shown, the first enthusiastic response was given to the idea of a society for Christian people who wanted to remain churched while seeking for the meaning of psychical manifestations more legitimately and deeply than was possible in either spiritualist or psychical research organisations. Whatever the original motivation, these were people who were not content to see human beings as animals with superior brains, or as programmed computers. Some came specifically for consolation in bereavement, with wounds to be dealt with apparently outside the scope of current church teaching. Some of the wounded sought intellectual satisfaction as well as comfort, and that, too, was part of the new society's brief. Some came seeking healing, or to learn about healing within the widest scope of the meaning of "spiritual". Many came with gifts of healing or of sensitivity (in the sense of attunement to the spiritual dimensions); these gifts had been shyly hidden from a deeply suspicious church and culture, and needed to be brought into the understanding, and use or relinquishment, of the possessor, whichever was better for wholeness of being. Many came because of a deep need for satisfaction for a questing mind which sought fulfilment of a need as real as that which might impel others to join musical, historical or other mutual interest societies.

It was, as has been said, the genius of the founders which led to the type of organisation set up for the newly formed Fellowship. It was seen from the start that there needed to be study groups all over the country, so that, however valuable the larger public meetings, the important rôle of the small local group was established; and it was continually stressed that the inspiration of these groups had to be Christian, and the subjects for study always linked back to Scriptural parallels and interpretations. Following those guidelines, individual members could remain firmly rooted in their own churches, of whatever denomination, while gaining a deeper understanding of the mysteries of the faith which in other circles were being phased out in the demythologising process begun in the nineteenth century and taken up so misguidedly and enthusiastically by the theologians of the mid-twentieth century.

So, in the second issue of the "News Sheet", in December 1954, there appeared an item under the title: "Study Groups" and headed: "This is perhaps the most important item in the 'News Sheet'. " The following text encouraged the setting up of groups wherever possible, the most important thing being "to find a Leader in each case who understands the real Christian position", and wherever possible local clergy members were seen as fulfilling that requirement. Details were to be co-ordinated centrally. The previous issue of the "News Sheet" had given some suggestions for study, and for reading, and this again was to be the recurring theme of guidance from the central council.

The period of growth now began, and dozens of groups were inaugurated across the country, from Doncaster in the North-East to Exeter in the South-West, and from Chelmsford in the East to Worcester in the West. Urban and country districts alike formed groups so that people were able to find one to contact or to be linked with, through an initial enquiry to the central office. CFPSS leaders travelled tirelessly to speak at local public or private meetings, and people with organisational talents began to be the founding members of local activities, thus further spreading the possibilities for growth and the setting up of strong groups country-wide.

It was soon realised that an officially recognised network of decentralisation could be very beneficial to the organic life of the Fellowship, and in 1957 the pattern of regional organisation was inaugurated. The announcement in the "News Sheet" for June 1957 gave the names of four areas and leaders, as follows: (1) Warwickshire, Worcestershire, Shropshire and Herefordshire (the Rev. Allan Barham); (2) Devon and Cornwall (Capt A.E. Hart); (3) Liverpool and Cheshire (Mrs L. Brown); and (4) Yorkshire (Mr R.S. Platt).

By September 1966, Col. Lester was able to report, at the South-West Conference in Torquay, that the country had been divided into eight regions, with 64 branches in the British Isles; and there were many smaller groups.[2] The branches were formally organised, with committees, minutes, annual reports, and formal speaker programmes, whereas the groups were more informal and were more likely to meet for study and prayer. Each region had a council, and the Regional Organisers were ex-officio members of the main Council. Regions organised local day conferences and retreats, making attendance possible for members who might not have been able to get to national occasions. Soon the great regional residential conferences, such as Torquay, Scarborough and Bournemouth were to be regular occurrences.

This form of regional organisation was to be one of the great strengths of the CFPSS. At a time when most clerical work had to be done by hand by volunteers, the regional organisers took over much of the administration which was proving too heavy for the central office, and subscriptions and the addressing and posting of the "Quarterly Reviews" became part of their responsibility until such time, much later, when modern technology made it a simpler matter for Head Office to take these functions back into its care.

However the contribution of regional and local workers was much more than administrative. First and foremost, local representatives (officially or as individuals) were able to be on-the-spot human contacts for those who might otherwise have thought themselves to be approaching merely a distant office. A welcome (by letter or telephone initially if necessary) would be followed up by an interview with help in dealing with whatever question or problem had been presented. This would be particularly appreciated by those suffering bereavement, or puzzled by an unusual and so far unexplained psychic experience, or troubled by something wrong encountered while searching for understanding. Not all those needing help would necessarily become members, but informal counselling would often lead to friendships being formed, and, in the majority of cases, to enrolment into the CFPSS with all that could mean of entering into a real fellowship.

Often the local representative would leave the name of an experienced and reliable member with the local library, where enquirers might look for a lead. Again a qualified person might, through local professional contacts, become involved in lectures to colleges or schools, or have the opportunity to work with church, hospice, bereavement or healing groups. The longer a group or branch was established the deeper would become the friendships between long-standing members, but always there would be the availability to those who might need occasional or one-off help or teaching. The Fellowship has never been a secret society and, like the Church, its whole purpose is to share its growing knowledge and understanding with any who might thereby find a need fulfilled.

Throughout its forty years there have been countless examples of unassuming voluntary workers carrying out all the chores and duties involved in any kind of regular meeting or occasional larger conference. To name all of these would be impossible, nor would they want it. Many names have become inseparably linked with a region or branch, often the meetings of the latter being held in a private home where host and hostess have combined friendship and generous hospitality with unremitting organisational work, in some cases for over thirty years. None of these would want public acknowledgement; it is enough to say that the continuation of the CFPSS to date has depended upon the enthusiasm and dedication of very many beyond those mentioned.

The impression might be given that there has never been dissension or division within the Fellowship. That would be an untrue picture. (See also Chapter 10). The very fact that the Fellowship offers opportunities for study and discussion of spiritual matters not normally considered in general church circles must result in its attracting seekers and enquirers who prize their independence, and who rebel against any suggestion that the regulation of CFPSS affairs should be based too closely on the disciplines of the churches themselves. Yet responsible CFPSS leaders have always needed to be aware of the danger in allowing those who do not regard themselves as church members to enter and dominate a group or branch and perhaps thus jeopardise the integrity of the founding inspiration.

These problems were very well dealt with in two related articles in issues of the "Quarterly Review" in 1980 and 1981. The author, Mr. Geoffrey West, an engineer, student of psychology and himself the centre of much family psychical communication, and an enthusiastic and dedicated supporter and promoter of the Fellowship's work, set out the problems met in striving for this balance of independence and loyalty to the original ideal.

He said: "We are a mixed group of people. Only a few of us are able to pursue profound studies. Many of us need a palatable diet of spiritual nourishment, and have found in the Fellowship fresh grounds for faith or simply fellowship in common certainties which we did not find in our home churches. Among those who approach us, it seems at least half are not likely to belong to a church. Are we to welcome them with strings of regulations while they are still tentatively moving from wonder to belief?"[3] And (in the second article)... "I can think of several persons who have never been members of the Fellowship but who pieced a broken life together again, helped by the love and prayers of a Fellowship group during a long period of attendance... This is the way we should pursue, not because there are no risks in it, but because risks are part of life and Jesus came that we might live more abundantly. Because of the risks there will be some bad cases, but bad cases make bad law. For a Christian the proper response to bad cases is prayer."[4]

One of the problems Mr West undoubtedly had in mind was a regulation originating from central office that non-members should only be permitted to attend three meetings without becoming members. This was, indeed, a rule more honoured in the breach than in the observance. It was also an example of the independence of groups and branches in their local methods which frequently caused tension if not dissension between those at the centre and those in the regions. Mostly these difficulties were worked through with good sense and forbearance. Sometimes real difficulties and occasionally maladministration caused branches to die or be closed down, but instances of this have been rare.

Independence caused one development to work its way to a natural and perhaps inevitable conclusion, in the breaking away, to set up its own Fellowship, by what was originally the "Scottish region", as it was still known and so described in the "Quarterly Review" of March 1967. Here Scotland was listed as one among other regions, its Organiser being the Rev. Hugh Martin of Glasgow. However, the newly formed and independent "CFPSS (Scotland)" held its first Council meeting in April, 1971 under the Chairmanship of the Rev. Hugh Martin, and Vice Chairman the Rev. John MacDonald. By 1980 CFPSS (Scotland) had decided to alter its constitution (originally based on that of the parent CFPSS), laying down terms of membership which required only that members should "wish to try to follow the teachings of Jesus". This deviation from the Trinitarian commitment of the parent Fellowship, while retaining a similar title, caused much concern, as expressed in Council meetings and reported in the "Quarterly Reviews" of the time.[5] Eventually, in 1989, after a ballot of members, the constitution of the CFPSS (Scotland) was changed back to the original wording, thus ending some years of dissension, with views being held strongly but sincerely on both sides, and perhaps illustrating the inevitable fluctuations brought about by differences of view and interpretation amongst lively and enquiring minds of varying denominations.

Many factors no doubt contributed to the original breaking away; and the eventual return to a common constitution was due not least to the efforts of successive chairmen of CFPSS (Scotland), the Rev. Dr David Hicks and the Rev. Angus Haddow. On this subject an interesting story can be read in a recent "Quarterly Review". This tells of the apparent post mortem intervention, in 1976, of the recently deceased founder, Col. Reginald Lester.[6] In this account, Mrs Lilianne Rich, a member of both Fellowships, tells of the occasion, at the 1976 Torquay Conference when, in the presence of Mrs Lester, she felt a "warm, unseen hand" on hers. Simultaneously, Grace Lester was sensing the presence of her late husband and his anxiety that the two Fellowships should be reconciled. Mrs Rich, a lady of practical wisdom and poetic sensitivity,[7] in due course made her contribution to the achievement of that desired objective. Meanwhile throughout its existence, despite doctrinal differences, the CFPSS (Scotland) has held many valuable conferences, retreats and branch meetings, and has continued to exchange publications and representatives with the parent CFPSS.

During this period, further away, overseas members had increased in numbers, in countries as widely different and apart as Canada, Australia, New Zealand, South Africa, Scandinavia and other parts of Europe. In many of these countries, branches flourished, and overseas events and personalities were a regular feature in the journal. This was especially so under the editorship of Reginald Lester whose journalistic work often took him abroad and enabled him to be instrumental in encouraging such growth.

In the United States very early interest in the newly formed Fellowship resulted in a visit to this country, in 1955, by a Mr Hening (sic) of the U.S.A. "primarily to collect information about the Fellowship in order that he may be instrumental in forming such a Fellowship in America."[8] Soon after, in the "News Sheet" of June 1956 the actual setting up of the Spiritual Frontiers Fellowship was reported as taking place, under the Rev. Paul Higgins, a Methodist minister, in Chicago. The Spiritual Frontiers Fellowship has continued to grow enormously over the years. It is now known as the Spiritual Frontiers Fellowship International, and has its separate academic society, the Academy of Religion and Psychical Research, which has something of the same relationship to the parent body as the "Christian Parapsychologist" has to the CFPSS. Frequent exchanges of speakers and journals between the CFPSS and the SFFI keep the links alive.

It is impossible to over-estimate the value of such exchanges of journals, and equally so of the domestic links established by regional newsletters and the CFPSS "house journal", the "Quarterly Review". The newsletters produced in the regions, the result of much hard work and thought on the part of the editors, provide local news of groups, branches and conferences, with very often additional information concerning compatible study and healing organisations and churches. The "Quarterly Review", as outlined in Chapter 2, first appeared as the "News Sheet" in September 1954. In that form and later as the "Quarterly Review" it had much of the character of newspaper reporting, not suprisingly in view of Col. Lester's journalistic background. Over the years it continued in that form, and then gradually changed into more of a magazine format but always carrying news of progress in regions, of important meetings, conferences and retreats, with ensuing reports, book reviews, correspondence, Annual General Meeting notices and reports. All this would be accompanied by regular features, such as the President's and Chairman's letters, together with articles on a wide variety of subjects relevant to CFPSS studies. Thus it has continued to constitute an important network of communication for members all over the country, valuable to all, but especially so for those not able to get to meetings or conferences.

Until his retirement in 1971, Col. Lester acted as editor, with, towards the latter years, the assistance of the Rev. Edna Rowlingson, a Congregationalist minister and enthusiastic group leader. From 1971 until 1983 an Editorial Board, with the General Secretary as Editor (first Mr Maurice Frost and later Mr Julian Drewett) carried the burden and responsibility of the four issues a year. (From 1977-78 Mr Frost and Mr Leslie Price acted as Joint Editors). Finally in the summer of 1983, the first issue under the Editorship of Dr Elizabeth Bowen appeared, and Dr Bowen has maintained the high preceding standard of content and raised it further over the years. The Fellowship owes a great debt of gratitude to her and to all the many other volunteers who have carried out the demanding work of keeping to publication dates over such a long period, and thus ensuring the continuity of the network of communication.

The title by which the CFPSS is affectionately known to its

members, "the Fellowship", perhaps best exemplifies this sense of networking which pervades all that is carried out in its name. Members, acquainted or otherwise, meet as friends, and the trust which is built up ensures that there is always someone available in any part of the country to undertake some work of helping or befriending. More will be written of this in the next and final chapter, especially of the rôle of the General Secretaries in this connection: for the moment let it be emphasised that the greatest strength of the "Fellowship" is implied in that informal title. Perhaps nowhere is this demonstrated more vividly than during the pilgrimages, which many members have been privileged to share and enjoy, to many places of sacred and historic Christian significance.

In the early days the Lesters and Miss Willie Van Dongen were responsible for leading several pilgrimages. (As a passing reference Miss Van Dongen was the author of an article describing the death of a Dutch child which illustrated most movingly the child's foreknowledge and shining faith in her Heavenly Father).[9] Iona was visited several times, with Assisi, Glastonbury, and Walsingham, among many other sites, and different leaders assuming the work of organising the journeys. In due course, Canon John Smith of Bristol, a supporter of the meditative and healing aspect of church worship, became involved, and eventually his name was to be synonymous with pilgrimage for Fellowship members. He has now led at least 12 pilgrimages to the Holy Land, and others to Assisi, the Oberammergau Passion Play and to Turin for the exposition of the Holy Shroud.

Writing of his time with the CFPSS, Canon John Smith explains that for him it has meant contacts "with many wonderful minds and kindred spirits, with the fascination also of meeting so many apparently quite ordinary people of average intelligence but who, in their own searching, had themselves been found, and this was very evident."[10] He speaks also of the humour to be found and shared within the Fellowship, and most of all on the pilgrim journeys where the mystery and sense of presence to be met in so many of the holy places alternate with the lightness of heart and joy which seem inseparable from the true pilgrimage.

This sense of the fine balance of seriousness of purpose and joy is something which is met at so many conferences and meetings, and underlines the impression that if indeed the whole of life for the Christian should be a pilgrimage, then in so much CFPSS activity the sense of moving on, rather than being static, is experienced, together with a true receiving of the "fruit of the spirit". Writing of his many memories of over thirty years of leading pilgrimages, John Smith finishes: "Perhaps pilgrimage is a valid expression of our search for God and determines the effort we make and our desire for that Sense of Presence that in the end overtakes us, and is realised as the great gift of God's grace and love that is the summit of all our seeking."[11]

This is a most apt expression of what so many members, over the past forty years, have found in belonging to the CFPSS.

CHAPTER 10

An Ongoing Fellowship

In the early chapters an account was given of the founding years of the CFPSS. Subsequent chapters dealt with different facets of the subjects studied, and in so doing related developments between those early years and now. However, some questions and matters have not been specifically considered, and to complete the story some of these perhaps should now be described, and brought up to date.

Even in a society devoted to such abstract concepts as psychical and spiritual studies, practical matters demand attention. They include financial affairs, premises, constitutional questions, and membership; and not one of these subjects is without its influence upon at least one of the others.

The question which over the years has generated the most interest and even emotional concern among Fellowship members is that of the establishing of an "Headquarters". From the very beginning this theme has recurred in the journals. The aim was to own some suitably impressive building in, naturally, London, where there would be a library, meeting rooms, offices and the opportunity for members to gather and even perhaps to stay, as if in a club. In the early days it was taken for granted that such premises would easily be obtained, through a gift or successful fund raising; but despite repeated attempts this goal was never reached.

Meanwhile the various offices, loaned, (out of London), and rented in London, some already described, were seen to be only temporary second-best alternatives. Even this less than satisfactory situation was found to be untenable when in 1971, following some well-meant but unfortunate mismanagement of finances, the Fellowship found itself unable to meet the proposed high rental increase for the offices in Denison House, Vauxhall Bridge Road. As a short-term expedient the newly appointed General Secretary, Mr Maurice Frost, offered a refuge in the office of his own business (a lecture agency) in Newman Street. Mr Frost had become assistant secretary in 1970, as well as Secretary to the World Fellowship Press, the publishing company for the Fellowship Book Club and recently taken over from the Rev. Cecil Gibbings, (see also p.78); and was in the process of attempting to regulate several matters which had got out of line before his taking over. However, even the accommodation he provided so generously, proved to be yet another insecure haven, as after 18 months a demolition order was imposed at very short notice.

At this point, the President, Chancellor Garth Moore, offered to share his small office and vestry at his historic Guild Church of St. Mary Abchurch in the City, and here the CFPSS administration and library (the latter itself subject to vicissitudes of housing), found a sanctuary for a few years. To be able to use the offices of such a church endowed the CFPSS with a base of much integrity at a kindly rental; but the din and clamour of seemingly never-ending demolition and rebuilding works in the adjacent city blocks rendered the last two years or so of occupancy an ordeal for the General Secretary (by now Mr Julian Drewett), and his voluntary helpers. Finally, the impending retirement of the Chancellor provided the culminating incentive to make other arrangements.

Meanwhile financial matters had been regulated through the efforts of Maurice Frost, and were now held in the care of a succession of hard-working and conscientious voluntary treasurers. Naturally the development of these matters included plans and discussions concerning the achievement of a permanent headquarters. In this matter a balance always had to be held between maintaining investment capital for income and the depletion that would follow the purchase of new premises, thus rendering the remaining capital incapable of supporting the upkeep of such premises, and other CFPSS commitments.[1]

Finally, after much research and consideration by a specially appointed Premises Committee, it was decided that rented administrative offices out of London would be a much more economical and viable concept for the future, especially as the holding of annual conferences around the country, and the visits of the General Secretary and Fellowship officers to regional conferences and local branches and groups, meant that nearly all other business with Head Office could easily be conducted by telephone or letter. Thus, despite the disappointed hopes of the minority who still had the vision of a prestigious central "Headquarters", the practice of an administrative office out of London, with a peripatetic General Secretary, was approved by Council and has worked well.

Membership numbers and appropriate subscriptions had to be brought into all calculations. In the very early days membership grew rapidly, reaching a reported peak of around 3,500 in 1974. By December 1976 the figure of 3,000 was reported, after which there was a dramatic reduction in the numbers quoted, until a figure of about 1,300 was given in 1982. There appears to have been some question as to the accuracy of the higher figures given in earlier years (over-stretched voluntary workers perhaps not realising the importance of accurate card-counting), but there was undoubtedly a dramatic drop around the late 1970s, due partly to general sociological reasons and partly to the tightening up of policy as described in Chapter 7. The more modest membership figure (which has remained consistent through the ensuing years) has always meant that the Fellowship's financial position has depended as much if not more on legacies and donations as on subscriptions, which latter, remaining low, have scarcely covered the cost of journals and postages, leaving all other expenses to be met out of investment income.

It would, of course, at any time have been very easy to increase membership if the subjects studied had been widened to include all the esoteric fringes of the subject labelled "psychic", with indiscriminate encouragement to members and enquirers to plunge headlong into the practice of psychical gifts and the investigation of phenomena. However, conforming always to the requirements of the Constitution and the Aims and Objects established when registering as a recognised charitable organisation, the leadership of the CFPSS has sought to maintain the highest standards of pastoral care and responsibility, within areas of theology consistent with membership of the churches included in the terms of membership. Some reference has already been made (in Chapters 7 and 9) to the unavoidable tensions which arose from time to time. In this present context it might be helpful to look at those conflicts in a little more detail.

The middle and late 1970s were the years of the rapid growth of many esoteric societies and interests, some occult, some coming under the blander description of 'New Age'. Many potential or actual CFPSS members were attracted by much of the subject matter dealt with in groups of this sort, and felt very strongly that these were subjects suitable for discussion and exploration within the CFPSS format. Others felt, equally strongly, that much of the material in question was outside the limits of CFPSS study, and to make it a subject of study would appear to authenticate it. Accordingly there was much controversy from time to time, reflected in articles and correspondence in the journals.[2] Eventually a policy was agreed upon, and harmony restored, at the cost of losing many would-be or existing members, but this was accepted by the Council as a necessary price to pay in maintaining the original aims of the founders, and of the implied contract in the inclusion of the word 'Churches' in the title.

Ironically, that title itself has always been the source of much pain and difficulty since, from the other end of the opposition, that is the fundamentalist churches, comes revulsion and distrust of the intent and purpose of the Fellowship, because of the use of the word 'Psychical'. Therefore, in 1973, not for the first time, alternatives were considered, and put to the membership for acceptance or rejection.[3] As always, the general consensus was that despite the debased usage of 'psychical' by so many outside the CFPSS, such critics only equating the word with the dark and evil side of the supernatural, it was in fact the soul content of the word which embodied the true ideal of the founders. So it was decided to keep the term 'psychical', while continuing to maintain that there is light and healing in the psyche as well as darkness.[4] For many it is an instantly recognisable word, often a life-line to those in sadness or trouble. It was also felt that it well illustrated the fact that no other Christian organisation offered the work and service which the CFPSS did. However there was and is a continuing price to pay in the restriction of would-be members and supporters who can not come to terms with the use of the word 'psychical'.

Eventually the Fellowship was to move into more peaceful waters, and even to find that the restraints on membership growth had come to be accepted as perhaps a providential steering towards the concept that instead of a fixed headquarters in London (where nowadays fewer and fewer people choose to go) the CFPSS must go out to the members. Together with the contribution of clergy and lay speakers from within the Fellowship and from outside, this has been largely achieved, following on from the establishing work of the Rev. Bertram Woods in the early years, through the work of the two salaried General Secretaries, Maurice Frost (1971-1980) and Julian Drewett (1981 to date).

Travelling around the country to annual and regional conferences and branch meetings, taking books and pamphlets for book-stalls, speaking on the work of the Fellowship, and meeting organisers and members, their work has made the greatest contribution imaginable to the continuity and coherence of the CFPSS. Each in his time as the one full-time, salaried member of the management team, has been responsible for the organising, issuing of proper notices, minuting and recording of Executive, Council and Annual General Meetings, and the implementing of all Council decisions. At Head Office, wherever that may have been, the General Secretary has been the contact and link not only for members but for all the very varied enquiries and appeals for help received from churches, media and the public in general.

Each has contributed through his own gift of sensitivity, which in the first place drew him into the Fellowship's orbit. In addition each has made an extra personal contribution. Maurice Frost steered the administration and membership through the stormy 1970s; and Julian Drewett, for several years Chairman of the Guild of Health, has added his own special experience of the ministry of healing and deliverance. His musicianship (as a professional church organist and choirmaster) has enhanced the programme at many annual conferences. To combine, as both have done, the gift of administration with other more subtle faculties, has for the past twenty years meant a rare and invaluable contribution to the Fellowship's work and continuance.

Meanwhile, some recurring questions seem to present

themselves for consideration. For instance, the Council is often asked: why doesn't the Fellowship publicise itself more? This question is asked with even more urgency when some enthusiastic new enquirer says (as happens quite frequently): "Why have I never heard of you before?"

First it must be said that judicious use of publicity is often made, as for instance with the advertising of conferences in the religious press, letters to editors, book reviews, and notices in libraries and diocesan or other denominational church clearing centres.[5] Apart from such notices, experience has taught the CFPSS to be very wary of other forms of advertising or publicity, for it has to be said, regretfully, that the majority of journalists, given the faintest whiff of the word 'psychic', will edit a report in such a way as to make the most sensational use of what was intended to be serious material. Policy for dealing with these problems was formulated in the very first year of the Fellowship's existence, as related in Chapter 2.

In 1959 this caution was justified in what may be described as the 'Panorama affair'. This is fully documented in the journals of the time, in which Col. Lester gave a full account of the making of a television programme, about the work of the Fellowship, and the biassed way in which he felt it had been presented.[6] Despite meticulous preparation by Col. Lester and the Council, and every assurance demanded and received that the presentation by the BBC would be fair and well-balanced, in the event the programme was seen to be biassed and tendentious, highlighting certain of the more sensational phenomena which formed only a small part of the Fellowship's enquiries. The articles include the letter of protest from the Council to Sir Ian Jacob, then Director General of the BBC, and his reply, and the other steps taken to overcome the adverse effect of the programme. In fact it would probably be inaccurate to refer to the incident as a disaster, as the BBC was inundated with letters of protest, and many letters of support and requests for membership were received by the Fellowship.

However, in 1965, continuing problems arising from clumsy publicity resulted in Col. Lester, an experienced journalist, setting out these difficulties and giving guidelines for branch secretaries, whilst announcing the appointment of Miss Oonagh

Robertson, also an experienced journalist, as Hon. Publicity Officer.[7] The current view remains that the greatest care needs to be taken at all times when dealing with the press and other media.

A beneficial form of indirect publicity has always been derived from the books and booklets produced by or for the Fellowship. In 1967 the CFPSS Book Club (a members' subscription project) was inaugurated, its first publication being "The Dissolving Veil" by Helen Greaves. It continued until 1974, its last production being Jane Sherwood's "Peter's Gate" (now republished by C.W. Daniel Co. Ltd.). Many worthwhile publications were produced in the years between, including "Life, Death and Psychical Research", already mentioned in Chapter 5. For a time the World Fellowship Press was owned as the CFPSS publishing company, but, as already related earlier in this chapter, this was unfortunately to fail through lack of expertise on the part of those involved, and its dissolution was another matter which the courageous Mr Frost had to oversee early in his tenure as General Secretary. However, although the Book Club and publishing company could not be continued, the practice of publishing its own material on a more modest scale has been maintained by the Fellowship with a good number of valuable booklets by members, most notably such as Dr Martin Israel and the Ven. Michael Perry. These reach many outlets, both religious and secular, and in all of them the title and aims of the CFPSS are established.

Another recurring question is that of working with younger people, and this matter has not been neglected over the years. Throughout its existence the CFPSS has responded to invitations for speakers to visit schools and colleges (including one unusual occasion when Col. Lester lectured to the cadets at the Royal Naval College, Dartmouth.[8]) There have been youth conferences, youth sections (with reduced membership subscriptions for students, which still apply), and a committee formed specifically to consider the question of the right approach to psychical and spiritual studies for younger people. As was mentioned in Chapter 8, a booklet on parapsychology in education was published. It has always been found that the subject evokes a lively response and sensible questions from younger people, but that in general they do not have the wish or time to devote themselves to any form of studious society, and the CFPSS has accepted that it is a resource but not a commitment for the younger generation. The study material produced by different Directors of Studies (G. Blaker, G. Whitby, B. Gadd and C. Hills in their turn), have made their own contributions to resources available, both for adult and student use, and lectures, articles, booklets and tapes have always kept the theme of study well to the forefront.

What then of those studies of matters psychical and spiritual? What still remains to be done? In 1965, Dr Leslie Weatherhead, an early and enthusiastic Fellowship supporter, wrote to congratulate the "Quarterly Review" on its 50th Jubilee Number. He said: "If there is one field of study and enquiry, not itself religious, which is relevant to religion, surely it is the field of psychical research? The New Testament opens with a story of angels singing about the birth of Christ. It closes with a picture of a life beyond death. It includes stories of telepathic communications, of evil spirits cast out, of contact with leaders who have been dead for centuries, and its culmination is the story of One who rose from the dead and appeared repeatedly afterwards. I prophesy that when this field is explored more fully by serious and trained investigators an immense enrichment of understanding will follow. I welcome warmly the work of the Churches' Fellowship." [9]

Considering these words, is the mission of the CFPSS to be regarded as accomplished? The answer is quite obviously "no", although the developments outlined in Chapter 8 suggest that there has been a classic case of the goalposts being moved; and, to carry the metaphor a little further, in playing on that enlarged pitch there has been some progress. "Allowing people to love their dead" (see Chapter 3) is an enormously significant development; the growth of the retreat movement and the practice of meditation and personal prayer is another encouraging sign; and the secular search for spiritual understanding (as in the study of the near-death experience) indicates a greater depth of awareness than might have been expected some twenty or thirty years ago.

None of this can be attributed directly to the work of the CFPSS, but every drop of water adds to the quality of the whole, even if changes are imperceptible at each stage. A religion based on the supernatural must believe in its source or prove to be founded on lies or superstition. The psychical or mystical content of the experiences of Christians so blessed must keep them faithful to the original inspiration. That has been and still is the witness of the CFPSS. Blessed indeed are those who have not seen and have yet believed, but in Jesus's reaction to Thomas's plea we are surely shown that God has a place for those who need to be convinced rationally as well as from inherent faith. (John 20, vv. 27 and 29). Summing up this interplay in an article in the "Christian Parapsychologist", Miss Renée Haynes finishes: "The two activities (religion and psychical research) need to be recognised as distinct in their own ends, means and terms of reference. Given this distinction, they have much to contribute to one another."[10]

Such a contribution is set out in a booklet by the Ven. Michael Perry on the spiritual implications of survival, in which he says: "The man who has treated every new venture into the unknown as an opportunity to put his hand into the hand of God and to go forth as a pilgrim will do the same on his journey into the unknown through death. The man who has not done so, and who has had no inkling of the spiritual implications of living, will find no spiritual implications of dying and will miss the spiritual implications of survival".[11]

It is interesting that the chosen motto of the CFPSS puts it in this order: "To faith add knowledge", implying that the search must be based on faith; that it is the work of a searching Christian, who is then willing to share that acquired knowledge and enhanced faith with others on the way. It is good, too, that the context of the motto, 2 Peter Chapter 1, v. 5, gives other qualities to be gained by effort, including, most importantly, goodness, which is listed between faith and knowledge. The search for knowledge must be based on faith and all that is good; it is thus that the Fellowship has been set its high standards, whether met or missed being for others to judge.

The President, the Rev. Dr Martin Israel, speaking at a Council retreat in July 1991, and basing his talk on 1 Peter, Chapter 1, reminded the Council that psychical studies, unless fully spiritualised, can be a cul-de-sac, with a form of dissociation occurring, through which some mediums operate, allowing spiritual energies or entities to enter which are completely undesirable. He went on to say that the justification for psychical studies is anthropological, leading to more understanding of human personality, consciousness, and all the related questions of survival. At the end of the Sermon on the Mount, Jesus felt it necessary to warn against false prophets; but with a sound Christian base ("not I, but Christ in me"), the CFPSS can continue to respond to other organisations, both religious and secular, who appeal for help.

There have been several references to bridge building throughout this history. Perhaps it is fitting to think that the work ahead for the CFPSS lies in continuing to strive for the establishing of those various bridges, that is between science and religion, medicine and healing, people in the churches and those outside, especially between the traditionalist churches and those people seeking a lost spirituality in New Age type societies. (As Michael Perry recounts in his latest book, "Gods Within", Dr Robert Runcie, when Archbishop of Canterbury, referring to New Age claims, "called on Christians to take it seriously 'in a spirit of engagement rather than of condemnation'."[12]) Not least bridges are needed in pastoral work between different dimensions, such as are encountered in the deliverance ministry as practised both by clergy and lay workers.

The 1980s and the early 90s have gradually revealed a trend towards many specialist societies having to accept diminishing membership, the reasons for this being far more attributable to sociological developments than to any decline in the validity of the work of those societies: the CFPSS has not been immune to this trend. At the same time it has watched the development within other organisations, not all of Christian inspiration, as well as within the churches, of deeper interest in and commitment to the ministry of healing, meditation and private spirituality, bereavement counselling, and other areas which were not so widely available when the Fellowship was first founded. As to an interest in psychical research and understanding, New Age societies have attracted those who prefer to follow such pursuits without the Christian basis required of CFPSS members.

All this must mean that potential members will probably remain fewer in number than before. However, there exists a great deal of work still to be done, and since those who do join the CFPSS are serious Christians there is no doubt that people of the right calibre will continue to find or be found by the CFPSS. It is heartening to know that the Fellowship is now soundly established in its administrative and financial organisation and above all in its adherence to the constitution and aims and objects, carefully formulated and registered with the Charity Commissioners. The experience and lessons learned in the past forty years, as described in this history, will not be wasted if the Fellowship can continue to make a valid contribution to the life and growth of the churches.

It is indeed still true to say, in the words of the Chairman, the Ven. Michael Perry, in his report to the Annual General Meeting at Digby Stuart College, Roehampton, in September 1988: "The Fellowship is in good shape and good heart to continue its work of counselling and supporting and justifying and forwarding an understanding of the psychic element within Christian life. Long may it witness to that indispensable aspect of Christian experience."[13]

In this context it is valid also to recall the words of the President, the Rev. Dr Martin Israel, in one of his Presidential letters in the "Quarterly Review:" "In a way the very use of the word 'spiritual' in the title of the Fellowship should be redundant, for are not the mainstream churches themselves the basis of spirituality? But in fact the mystical side of our faith is little acknowledged by many traditional church people, and it is good that there should be a group interested in the point of intersection between the mystical and the spiritual. Such a terrain is very much our own, hence my enthusiastic service to our Fellowship."[14]

This seems to be the core of the commitment of all Fellowship members. There is a conviction that is at the heart of each individual member's faith, a conviction of the reality and vital importance of that intersection of the mystical and spiritual, and of the psychical. As Christians believing in the Communion of Saints, members know there is no need to fear whatever manifestations may occur in these occasions for intersection. Their concern is intellectual as well as spiritual, pastoral as well as personal. Where they can help others they do, and they know that whatever is beyond them can be referred to someone more experienced or knowledgeable. They know, too, that they are "encompassed about with a great cloud of witnesses" (Heb. Chapter 12, v.1), an extension of the earthly network of fellow Christians, and that it is their joy to work within that great Christian communion of earth and heaven, and their task to share that joy with fellow Christians and to help non-Christians to come into such joy.

So the Churches' Fellowship for Psychical and Spiritual Studies, a society of Christians dedicated to the study of the gifts of the Spirit as set out in the New Testament (I Cor. Chapter 12) and exemplified in numerous other references throughout the scriptures, celebrates its fortieth anniversary, and re-dedicates itself to continue in the work, remembering always to seek for those other signs of which the New Testament speaks in Galatians Chapter 5, v. 22, the fruit of the Spirit, love, peace, joy and other attributes of a humanity in tune with its saviour, Jesus Christ.

APPENDIX A (i)

The Churches' Fellowship for Psychical Study
President: The Hon. Sir Cyril Atkinson, LL.D.
Vice-President: The Rev. Canon W.S. Pakenham-Walsh, M.A.
Hon. Secretary: The Rev. G. Maurice Elliott
    46, Lyford Road, London, S.W.18

                                  4, CURSITOR HOUSE,
                                        CURSITOR STREET,
                                              LONDON, E.C.4.
                                  Telephone Holborn 2441

AIMS AND OBJECTS (1954)

The above Fellowship of Clergy, Ministers and Lay-people of all Christian Denominations has been formed to encourage the study, within the Churches, of the known facts of Psychic Science.

The Fellowship believes that the gifts of the Holy Spirit to the Church, which is the "blessed company of all faithful people" are meant to be permanent and exercised *to-day* (see 1 Cor., 12); and that 'seers' and 'sensitives' are with us *to-day* and that their gifts should be dedicated to the service of God and Mankind.

The Fellowship aims at making its existence known, and carrying out its investigations and activities, in the following way:

1. By Announcements in the Press – Secular and Religious.
2. By arranging for public lectures, and, we hope, for sermons.
3. By the holding of Meetings, both large and small (in halls, drawing-rooms, etc.), which Meetings shall always be opened with prayer, the objects of such Meetings being to enlighten the general public and to form branches of the Fellowship in cities, towns and villages throughout the country.
4. By individual study, thought and prayer.
5. By the creation and circulation of psychical literature on the highest level of spiritual, intellectual and scientific integrity.
6. By stressing the importance of the element of Communion with the Unseen World in Public Worship, United Prayer, and in participation in the Holy Communion Service.

7. By the care and development of psychic gifts.
8. By affording the opportunity for members to consult tested, trusted Christian 'sensitives' dedicated to God for this purpose.

APPENDIX A (ii)

(Extract from the Constitution, as revised in 1973)

3. (i) The objects of the Fellowship are to encourage the study, within the Christian churches, of spiritual or paranormal or psychological and other scientific phenomena and to try to assess their validity and their relevance to the Christian faith.

   (ii) Without prejudice to the generality of the foregoing, the Fellowship may organise or take part in conferences and meetings and may publish literature and organise and support research and study meetings and shall with circumspection encourage the fostering by individuals of spiritual and paranormal gifts. Other than its common Christian faith, which is of its essence, the Fellowship holds no corporate views and it may at the discretion of the Council co-operate with and affiliate to other bodies in pursuit of the Fellowship's objects and shall endeavour to co-operate and work with the Christian Churches which belong to or are affiliated to the World Council of Churches.

APPENDIX B

The Churches' Fellowship for Psychical Study
4, Cursitor House, Cursitor Street, London E.C.4
President: The Hon. Sir Cyril Atkinson, LL.D.
Vice-President: The Rev. Canon W.S. Pakenham-Walsh, M.A.

Hon. Vice-Presidents:

The Bishop of Peterborough	Lady Howarth
The Bishop of Ripon	The Rev. Canon A. Oswald Jones
The Dean of St. Paul's	Hon. Mrs. Herbert Lane
Lady Atkinson	The Dowager Lady Lawson-Tancred
Lady Becke	Lady Liddell
Sir Alfred Bossom, M.P.	F. Brodie Lodge, Esq.
The Rev. Canon R.J. Campbell	Baron E. Palmstierna, G.C.V.O.
The Rev. Canon Edward Carpenter	The Rev. Canon T.P. Stevens
The Rev. Canon E.T. Davies	The Rev. Canon Mervyn Stockwood
Lady Fforde	Rev. Dr. Leslie Weatherhead
Lady Harrington	The Rev. Canon A.F. Webling
The Hon. John Henniker	The Hon. Mrs. Berkeley Williams

Hon. Secretary and Treasurer:
The Rev. G. Maurice Elliott
46 Lyford Road, London, S.W.18

Dear

We thank you for your letter and are glad to know of your interest in the Fellowship, and we have pleasure in sending you particulars of our Aims and Objects.

You will, we are sure, be interested to know how the C.F.P.S. came into being. Lt.-Col. Reginald M. Lester, author of "In Search of the Hereafter," invited a few clergymen whom he knew to be interested in psychical research to meet him with a view to the formation of a Fellowship *within the Christian Churches* of all Christians who wished to know more of psychical phenomena, past and present, their value, meaning and purpose. We met, formed ourselves into a temporary committee, and set to work. The first thing we had to do was to obtain the support of some Church Leaders. This we did with remarkably good results. The next thing was to publish in the secular and religious Press the news that "The Churches'

Fellowship for Psychical Study" was now in existence and had the full support of well-known Churchmen.

Now we are hoping that you and others will quickly rally round us so that together – you and we – may make the work of this Fellowship a boon and a blessing to an ever increasing number of Christian men and women.

We have, as yet, only small funds, for we are only at the beginning of things, but we are confident that God will provide all things necessary by inspiring those who realise the importance of such a Fellowship to give according as He has prospered them.

We sincerely hope that you will join us and complete and return the enclosed Membership Form.

(1954) Yours sincerely,

(Hon. Secretary)

NOTES

Notes

1 "Angels in Dark Places" Beryl Statham: Churchman Publishing in association with the CFPSS 1990.

Chapter 1

1 "Psychic Studies: A Christian's View", Michael Perry, Aquarian Press 1984.
2 "Whole in One", David Lorimer, Arkana 1980.
3 "Life After Life", Raymond A. Moody, Bantam Press, New York, November 1976.
   "Reflections on Life after Life", Raymond Moody, Corgi 1978.
4 "The Christian Healing Ministry", Morris Maddocks, SPCK 1981.
5 "Quarterly Review", December 1989 (pp. 18 and 32).

Chapter 2

1 "Lang, Temple and the origin of the 1939 Report" – René Kollar – "Christian Parapsychologist" June 90, Vol. 8, No. 6, p. 204 (See also Chapters 3 and 5).
2 "Quarterly Review", March 1961, p. 3.
3 Geo. G. Harrap & Co., 1952.
4 Appendix A.
5 Appendix B.
6 "Quarterly Review", December 1960, p.7.
7 "Quarterly Review", September 1959, p.1.
8 See Chapter 3.
9 See Chapter 4.
10 "Quarterly Review", March 1963, p.1.

Chapter 3

1 "The Christian Hope – Eternal Life", an address by Canon John D. Pearce-Higgins read to the 49th Annual Conference of the Modern Churchmen's Union, August 1966.
2 "Requiem Healing; A Christian Understanding of the Dead" by Michael Mitton and Russ Parker, Daybreak, London (DLT), 1991.
3 "Liturgy and Worship", Ed. W.K. Lowther Clarke, DD, SPCK, 1964.
4 "Anglican Worship Today" (Collins Illustrated Guide to the ASB, 1980), Ed. Buchanan, Lloyd and Miller, Grove Books, 1980.
5. "Christian Parapsychologist", June 1991.
6 "Light", CPS, Summer 1979.

7   See Chapter 5 for further reference.
8   "The Supreme Adventure", Robert Crookall, CFPSS (James Clarke), 1961.
9   "Testimony of Light", Helen Greaves (now pub. C.W. Daniel, Saffron Walden).
10 "The Christian Healing Ministry", Morris Maddocks, SPCK, 1981.
11 "Quarterly Review", December 1963.
12 "Quarterly Review", Autumn 1983.

Chapter 4

1. "The Christian Healing Ministry", Morris Maddocks, SPCK, 1981.
2   Ibid.
3   (Obituary) "Quarterly Review", December 1966.
4   "Deliverance" – The Christian Exorcism Study Group (ed. Michael Perry), SPCK, 1987.
5   "Exorcism and the Fellowship", E. Garth Moore, M. Israel, M. Frost, "Quarterly Review", September 1975.
6   "The Healing Miracles of Wesley", the Rev. F.R. Sydenham, "Quarterly Review", September 1979.
7   "A Modern Miracle", D.A. Owen, "Quarterly Review", September 1985.
8   "Quarterly Review", March 1962.
9   "Healing and the Fellowship", Maurice Frost, and "The Practice of Spiritual Healing", Martin Israel, "Quarterly Review", December 1976.

Chapter 5

1   Rhea White, Bibliographer, Editor of "Exceptional Human Experience", Pub. The Parapyschology Sources of Information Centre, N.Y.
2   "Quarterly Review", December 1959, p.12.
3   "News Sheet", March 1955, p.3.
4   "News Sheet", December 1955, p.8. See also "The Imprisoned Splendour", R. Johnson, Hodder and Stoughton, 1953.
5   "News Sheet", March 1956, p.7.
6   Frances Banks, "Frontiers of Revelation", Max Parrish, 1962; Allan Barham "Quarterly Review", 1965-66 and 1967-69.
7   "Quarterley Review", March 1964, December 1966, December 1969, March 1970 and June 1967 respectively.
8   "Life, Death and Psychical Research", Rider, 1973.
9   Obit, "Quarterly Review", June 1985, p.2; December 1969 p.35, and September 1986, p.21 respectively.
10 And see: "Quarterly Review", September 1987: "Communication and Communion", O. Tomkins.
11 "Death Has No Sting", Florence West Pell, CFPSS, 1972.
12 "Testimony of Light", Helen Greaves, (Chapter 3, Note 9).
13 "The Times", 3rd May 1969.
14 "Christian Parapsychologist", March 1979 (Full Report and comment by E. Garth Moore), June 1979, M. Perry, June 1990, R. Kollar.
15 "The Churches and Psychical Research", A. Haddow: "Christian Parapyschologist", December 1980.
16 "Quarterly Review", September 1982.
17 See Chapter 1, Notes 2 and 3.

18 Charles Fryer, "A Hand in Dialogue", James Clarke, 1983 and "Geraldine Cummins – An Appreciation", Pilgrim Books, 1990.
19 "Quarterly Review", September 1983 and December 1983.
20 Allan Barham, "Strange to Relate", Colin Smythe, 1980 and "Life Unlimited", Voltura Press, 1982.
21 See Note 1 (Vol. 8, December 1990).

Chapter 6

1 "Frontiers of Revelation", Frances Banks, Max Parrish, 1962 (p.24).
2 Ibid., p.26.
3 Ibid., p.27.
4 "Teach Them to Live", Frances Banks, Max Parrish, 1958.
5 "Quarterly Review", December 1963, p.7.
6 "Precarious Living", Martin Israel, Hodder and Stoughton, 1976, p.52.
7 Vera Staff: an unpublished MS.
8 "Four Studies in Mysticism", Frances Banks (out of print).
9 "Remembered on Waking", Vera S. Staff, CFPSS, 1975.

Chapter 7

1 Minutes of Council Meeting, 10th October 1956.
2 "Quarterly Review", March 1977, Canon J.D. Pearce-Higgins, "The Start of a Pilgrimage".
3 "Nothing to Hide", Leonard Argyle, CFPSS, 1970.
4 "Quarterly Review", September 1970: "The CFPSS and the Churches", B. Bunce.
5 "Quarterly Review", December 1972: "The Fellowship at the Crossroads", A. and M. Virgin (See also Chapters 9 and 10).
6 See "The Occult", Colin Wilson, Mayflower, 1971.
7 "About Bereavement", B. Bunce and B. Statham, CFPSS, 1983.
8 "The Resurrection of Man", Michael Perry, Mowbrays, 1975.
9 "The Christian and the Supernatural", Morton T. Kelsey, Search Press London, 1977.
10 "Quarterly Review", Summer 1987, Chairman's Letter.
11 "If The Trumpet Give An Uncertain Sound", J.D. Pearce-Higgins, CFPSS, 1957.

Chapter 8

1 "Psychology's Impact on the Christian Faith", Edward C. Barker, Allen and Unwin, 1964.
2 "Quarterly Review", September 1966. Report by J.D. Pearce Higgins.
3 "The Oxford Companion to the Mind", 1987, Professor John Beloff – "Parapsychology and the Mind-Body Problem".
4 Michael Perry, "The Christian Parapsychologist", March 1979, p.35.
5 Martin Israel, "The Quarterly Review", Summer 1989 (p.26).
6 "The Quarterly Review", June 1959.
7 "The Hidden Springs", Renée Haynes (p.149), Hollis and Carter, 1961.
8 "The Quarterly Review", Winter 1982. Report of Annual General Meeting.
9 "The Necessity of Parapsychology", Max Payne – CFPSS Ecumenical Conference on Christian Parapsychology, September 1990 (CFPSS Cassette) (See also, "Christian Parapsychologist", June 1992).

Chapter 9

1. "Fifteen Years of the Churches' Fellowship", R.M. Lester, SFF Journal, Summer 1969.
2. "Quarterly Review", December 1966 – Conference Report.
3. "Quarterly Review", Winter 1980, G. West, "Regulating the Fellowship I".
4. "Quarterly Review", Spring 1981, G. West, "Regulating the Fellowship II".
5. "Quarterly Review", Summer and Autumn 1980.
6. "The Reassuring Hand", L.G. Rich, "Quarterly Review", June 1992.
7. "Echo of Many Voices", L.G. Rich, Aberdeen University Press, 1980.
8. "News Sheet", June 1955. See also "Quarterly Review", September 1963, "Mr. Hening" was probably the Rev. Ralph Henard, now (1963) Vice President of SFF.
9. "Preparing for a Journey", W. Van Dongen, "Quarterly Review", September 1967.
10. Letter – John Smith to Barbara Bunce.
11. "A Sense of Presence", John Smith, "Quarterly Review", December 1991.

Chapter 10

1. "Quarterly Review", December 1973: "From the General Secretary", Maurice Frost.
2. "Quarterly Reviews", December 1972: "The Fellowship at The Crossroads", A. and M. Virgin, June '78: "Maurice Frost Replies", M. Frost, December 1978: "The Chairman's Letter", M. Israel; Summer 1982: "Some Reflections on Our Present Discontents", A. and M. Virgin.
3. "Quarterly Review", March 1973: "From the President", E.G. Moore.
4. "Quarterly Review", December 1973. Chairman's Report at Annual General Meeting, K. Cuming.
5. "Quarterly Review", June 1982: General Secretary's Notes, Julian Drewett.
6. "Quarterly Review", December 1959 and March 1960.
7. "Quarterly Review", June 1965.
8. "Quarterly Review", March 1969.
9. "Quarterly Review", December 1966.
10. "Christian Parapsychologist", March 1977: "Religion and Psychical Research", Renée Haynes.
11. Christian Parapsychology Papers No. 2: "The Spiritual Implications of Survival", Michael Perry.
12. "Gods Within: A Critical Guide to the New Age", Michael Perry, SPCK, 1992.
13. "Quarterly Review", December 1988.
14. "Quarterly Review", March 1987.

INDEX

(Figures in brackets denote references in chapter notes where the names have not appeared in the text)

A

Academy of Religion and Psychical Research, 68.
Alister Hardy Research Centre (Religious Experience Research Unit), 53.
All Souls, Guild of, 22.
American Association for the Advancement of Science, 55.
Anglican (See Church of England).
Archbishops' Commission on Divine Healing, 30.
Argyle, Leonard, 51.
Ash, Dr Michael, 32.
Atkinson, Sir Cyril, 13, 19.
Augustine, St, 4.

B

BBC, 77.
BMA, 31.
Bacon, Gwen, 57.
Banks, Frances, 19, 26, 36, 38, 41-46, (89).
Baptist (Church), 28.
"Baptist Times", 50.
Barbanell, Maurice, 35.
Bardsley, Bishop Cuthbert, 13.
Barham, Rev. Allan, 36-39, 58, 64, (89).
Barker, Rev. Edward, 55.
Bearman, H.V., 37, 38.
Beloff, Prof. John, 56.
Bendit, Dr Laurence, and Phoebe, 34.
Bennett, Rev. George, 28.
Bignall, C.E., 46.
Birkett, Lord, 43.
Blaker, George, 37, 39.
Bowen, Dr Elizabeth, 69.
Bretherton, Rev. Donald, 36, 51.
Brice-Smith, Margaret, 57, 58.
Brown, Mrs L., 64.
Bunce, Barbara, (90).
Burrswood (see Kerin),
Butler, Edwin, 58.

C

CPS (College of Psychic Studies), 9, 24, 46, 57.
Case, Enid 39.
Charity Commissioners, 82.
Christian Deliverance Study Group (formerly Christian Exorcism Study Group), 32.
Christian Science, 9.
Church of England/Anglican, 7, 21, 23, 24, 27, 45, 48, 57.
Church of England Liturgical Commission, 23.
"Church Times", 22, 26.
Churches Council on Divine Healing, 30.
Clarke, W.K. Lowther, (88).
"Clergy Review", 60.
Cluny, 23.
Coggan, Archbishop Donald, 28.
Collins, Illustrated Guide to the ASB, (88).
Communion of Saints, 3, 25, 31, 33, 82.
Community of the Resurrection, 42.
Constitution, 95.

Compton, Mrs S.H., 14, 16.
Congregational, 69.
Corbett, Capt. Hugh, 61.
Cuming, Rev. Dr Kenneth, 32, 45, 52, (91).
Cummins, Geraldine, (90).
Curtis, Fr. Geoffrey, 24.
Cranmer, Thomas, 23.
Creator, 26.
Crookall, Dr Robert, 25, 35.

D

"Daily Herald", 30.
"Daily Mail", 30.
Dowding, Lord, 10.
Drewett, Julian, 69, 73, 76 (91).

E

Eastaugh, Bishop Cyril, 22.
Elliott, Rev. Maurice, 11-13, 15-18, 25, 30, 49.
Elliott, Irene, 11, 25.
Ellis, David, 58.
Evangelical, 22, 53.
Evans, Dr Griffiths, 31, 36.
"Expository Times", 60.

F

Fatima, 33, 47.
Field, Olive, 14.
Ford Robertson, Dr W., 31.
Francis of Assisi, St, 47.
Frost, Maurice, 33, 52, 58, 69, 73, 76, 78, (89), (91).
Fryer, Rev. Charles, 39.

G

Gadd, Barbara, 60, 79.
Gibbings, Rev. Cecil, 73.
Glazewski, Canon Andrew, 37.

God, 3, 4, 8, 26, 30, 31, 33, 41, 44, 45, 54, 71, 80.
Greater World Christian Spiritualist Church, 13.
Greaves, Helen, 25, 38, 78.

H

Habgood, Archbishop John, 1, 4, 5.
Haddow, Rev. Angus, 39, 53, 67.
Hall, Rev. Richard, 46.
Harper, Rev. Michael, 51.
Harrington, Rev. Charles, 12.
Hart, Capt. A.E., 64.
Haynes, Renée, 59, 60, 80.
Health, Guild of: 32, 76.
Hening (and see Henard), 68.
Henard, Rev. Ralph, (91).
Hicks, Rev. Dr David, 67.
Hickson, Rev. James Moore, 28.
Higgins, Rev. Paul, 68.
Hills, Christine (Frost), 79.
Holy Spirit, ii, 11, 33, 41, 46, 48, 51, 83.
Howson, Rev. V. and Mrs, 14.

I

IANDS (International Association of Near-Death Studies) – see Lorimer.
Institute of Journalists, 17.
Institute of Religion and Medicine, 32.
Israel, Rev. Dr Martin, 4, 6, 12, 25, 32-3, 41, 44-47, 52, 57, 78, 80, 82, (89), (91).

J

Jacob, Sir Ian, 77.
Jesus Christ, ii, 23, 26, 41, 45, 48, 49, 52, 54, 66, 79, 80, 81, 83.
John of the Cross, St, 46.
Judaism, 44, 45.

K

Kelsey, Rev. Morton, 53.
Kennaby, Rev. K., 19.
Kerin, Dorothy, 28, 31, 33, 45.
Kollar, Rev. René, (88), (89).

L

LSA (see CPS).
Lambeth Conference, 9, 28.
Lang Report/Commission: 10, 24, 39, 56, (88).
Lester, Reginald, 10-15, 17, 18, 30, 31, 35, 40, 50, 51, 62, 64, 68, 69, 70, 77, 78.
Lester, Grace, 16, 18, 68, 70.
Lewis, Michael, 58.
"Light", 24.
Lindbeck, George, 4.
Lodge, Brodie, 16.
Lorimer, David, 6.
Lourdes, 33.

M

McDonald, Rev. John, 18, 67.
Maddocks, Bishop Morris, 26, 28, 53, (88).
Magee, Rev. Max. 56.
Maidstone Prison (Maidstone, Experiment), 43.
Mandus, Brother, 33.
Martel, Linda, 33.
Martin, Rev. Hugh, 67.
Mary (Our Lady), 23.
Matthews, Rev. Dr W.R., 13, 18, 30, 35, 48, 49.
Methodist (Church), 7, 14, 18, 25, 28, 68.
Mitchell, John, 6.
Mitton, Rev. Michael, 22.
Moody, Dr Raymond, 6, 39.
Moore, Chancellor E. Garth, 19, 26, 31, 37, 39, 49, 52, 73, (89), (91).

N

Nazis, 45.
Near-Death Experience (see Lorimer, Moody).
New Age, 27, 52, 53, 75, 81.

O

Oddie, Rev. William, 27.
Owen, Dorothy, (89).

P

Padre Pio, 33, 59.
Pakenham-Walsh, Canon W., 12, 13.
"Panorama", 77.
Parapsychology Foundation, N.Y., 55.
Parapsychology Sources of Information Centre, N.Y., (89).
Parker, Rev. Russ, 22.
Payne, Prof. Max. 61.
Pearce-Higgins, Canon John, 12, 15, 17, 22, 30, 34, 36, 38, 49, 50, 54, 55, 58, 60.
Pell, Florence West, 38.
Percival, Evelyn, 37.
Perry, Ven. Michael, 4, 5, 7, 8, 24, 25, 32, 53, 54, 56, 59, 60, 78, 80, 81, 82, (89).
Platt, R.S., 64.
Plotinus, 46.
Price, Leslie, 57-60, 69.
"Psychic News", 35.

R

Reformation, 21, 23.
Religious Experience Research Unit – see Alister Hardy.
Ramsey, Archbishop Michael, 19, 28.
Raynor Johnson, Prof., 35, 57.

Rich, Lilianne, 68.
Roberts, Rev. Selwyn, 16, 26, 30.
Robertson, Oonagh, 78.
Robinson, Bishop John, 22.
Roman Catholic, 7, 27.
Rosher, Grace, 36.
Rowlingson, Rev. Edna, 69.
Runcie, Archbishop Robert, 81.

S

SPR (Society for Psychical Research), 9, 11, 29, 34, 56, 60, 61.
SPR Cambridge, 19.
Sai Baba, 59.
Scientific and Medical Network, 32, 37, 38.
Scotland (CFPSS), 52, 56, 67, 68.
Scotland, Church of, 7, 56.
Shaw, Wilfred, 37.
Sherwood, Jane, 78.
Simpson, Rev. F.S.W., 10, 12, 15, 16.
Smith, Rev. Canon John, 7, 70, 71.
Somme, Battle of, 10, 21.
Spirit Holy – see H.
Spiritual Frontiers Fellowship, 68.
Spiritualism, 9, 10, 18, 24, 29, 30, 35, 39, 49, 56, 62.
Staff, Vera, 46.
Statham, Beryl, ii, (90).
Stockwood, Bishop Mervyn, 38, 39.
Sydenham, Rev. F.R., (89).
Sydney, Jean, 46, 58.
Swedenborg, Emanuel, 59.

T

Teilhard de Chardin, P., 46.
Temple, Archbishop William, 28, (88).

Teresa of Avila, St, 46.
"Theology", 60.
Theosophy, 9.
Thérèse of Lisieux, St, 47.
Thomas, St, 80.
Tomkins, Bishop Oliver, (89).

U

Underhill, Bishop Francis (Underhill Report), 10, 24, 39.
United Reformed Church, 28.

V

Van Dongen, Willie, 70.
Vivian, Gwen, 14, 34.
Virgin, Rev. Alun and Margaret, 32, 39, 51, 52, (91).

W

Weatherhead, Rev. Dr Leslie, 13, 28, 79.
Wesley, John, 33.
West, Geoffrey, 66.
Westall, Bishop Wilfrid, 50.
White, Alice, 14, 15, 16.
White, Rhea, 34, 40.
Whitby, Rev. George, 37, 79.
Wilkins, Rev. W.T., 37.
Wilson, Colin, (90).
Wilson, Rev. M., 14.
Witchcraft, 53.
Woods, Rev. Bertram, 18, 25, 31, 76.
World Council of Churches, 14, 48, 85.
World Fellowship Press, 73, 78.